# THE BUSINESS OF THE MIND

MONTHLY DEVOTIONAL

# THE BUSINESS OF THE MIND

A 12-MONTH JOURNEY INTO HOW TWO MEN OVERCAME INTERNAL CHALLENGES, AND WITH GOD'S HELP, BUILT GREATER SELF-CONFIDENCE.

LARRY D. YARBROUGH, SR.
*and* TIMOTHY JOHNSON

truth

Published by Truth Publications, LLC
www.truth-brand.com

The Business of the Mind
Copyright © 2022 by Truth Publications, LLC

All rights reserved. No part of this book may be reproduced without written consent from Truth Publications, LLC.

Cover Design: Truth Publications, LLC
ISBN: 978-1-7366112-3-4

# TABLE OF CONTENTS

*Acknowledgments* ........................................................................... i

*Introduction* ................................................................................... v

*Fasting* .......................................................................................... ix

Month 1 | Laying the Foundation ........................................... 1

Month 2 | Fruit and Root ........................................................ 15

Month 3 | On These Things .................................................... 45

Month 4 | Establishing Your Worth ...................................... 65

Month 5 | The Life and Journey ............................................ 73

Month 6 | "23" ......................................................................... 125

Month 7 | Weak but Willing ................................................... 149

Month 8 | Stay Connected ...................................................... 169

Month 9 | Living It .................................................................. 183

Month 10 | Process before Purpose ....................................... 199

Month 11 | Seasons and Assignments .................................... 229

Month 12 | Predestined ............................................................ 251

Additional References ............................................................. 261

# ACKNOWLEDGMENTS

First and foremost, I give all glory and honor to my Lord and Savior, Jesus Christ. Without Him, achieving this milestone would not be a reality. I desire to please my Heavenly Father, God, with all that I am and all He blesses me to do.

Next, to my beautiful and precious wife, I love you with all my heart! Thank you for being my biggest encourager and supporter. I married you 21 years ago, and I would not change our meeting, falling in love, or becoming one. God shows me daily how much He loves me by allowing me to share life with you! My affections for you go beyond what words can express. Thank you for being the wife of my dreams. To my sons, Larry D., Jr., (L.J.) and Lance: I love you both. When I look at you, I see the love of God. It is because of you guys that my life is fun and exciting. You both are my heroes!

Thirdly, I am indebted to my co-author, Timothy R. Johnson. I clearly remember our first professional encounter. Before you and your lovely wife united with the Changing Lives Ministries Church family, you pitched something to me, and I decided to go with someone else. Isn't life funny? I never imagined we would author a book together. I am also in awe of how God used you to push me to something like this project, especially as laid back as you are. I appreciate you as a human being, a man of God, a professional, and your willingness to serve! God put us together for this day and time. I pray God's blessing over you, your wife, and your sons.

I would like to acknowledge Changing Lives Ministries Church (CLM). We are family! Thank you for your prayers and support! To

## ACKNOWLEDGEMENTS

my parents, Mr. Larry W. and Mrs. Jessie Yarbrough, I am grateful to the Lord for the Godly upbringing you provided. My spiritual parents, Mr. Alphonso and Mrs. Monique Montgomery, God knew I needed you both in my life. You are both gifts to me, my family, and the Kingdom of God.

Finally, my prayer is that you (the readers) will be positively impacted and changed for the better.

# INTRODUCTION

### The Business of the Mind

*The Business of the Mind* is an interactive yearly devotional that, when completed, will help shape the reader's perspective for each new day. The format of this devotional is unique in that it does not provide a separate devotion for each day of the year. Instead, it provides a format that allows the reader to complete the entire devotional within a year without being committed to just one book throughout the year. The reader can begin this devotional at any month throughout the year and at nearly any time within a month. Since this devotional does not cover 365 days of material, the reader also can supplement with a traditional 365-day devotional on those days when the reader is not engaged in this particular devotional.

The information shared in this devotional is intended to help readers overcome obstacles, reach milestones, and conquer their internal fears and insecurities by putting God's Word into practice. The concept of this devotional originated as one of the authors was intentional with combating insecurities and low self-esteem, so he focused on building a strong mind. Throughout an 18-month journey, he went through a series of fasting, prayer, and study of God's Word that helped him gain greater confidence and a more positive self-image. From there, he set out to accomplish goals that, prior to this journey, were milestones he thought were out of his reach. To help bring this information to readers, the lead author, having overcome certain

# INTRODUCTION

insecurities, fears, and health battles of his own, further studied and developed the 12 months of material that will be shared in this devotional.

To receive the full effect of this devotional, it is encouraged that the reader follows along with the fasting, praying, and studying that is offered each month. It is important to note that neither author is, nor claim to be, medical professionals. Therefore, be sure to consult with a healthcare provider before beginning any exercise routine or altering any diet regimes.

On each day of this study, the reader is encouraged to take time in the morning (earlier than usual, sacrificing sleep, or later at night to prepare for the next day) to go through the process of this study. The reader should be sure to reflect throughout the day on the readings. The Lord may allow specific individuals to cross paths with the reader throughout the days of the study. Awareness of these moments and the things the Lord may be trying to reveal is essential. Also, the reader should be open to the idea of sharing time with others (meals, conversations, etc.) as a way of being available to hear from God through someone else.

Discipline and consistency are two primary keys in this devotional. It will require the reader to be disciplined to stay consistent throughout this study. Although this devotional allows for days off, it is essential to keep seeking God throughout the breaks in this journey.

¹²"In those days when you pray, I will listen. ¹³If you look for me wholeheartedly, you will find me. ¹⁴I will be found by you," says the LORD.

Jeremiah 29:12-14a NLT

# FASTING
### The Business of the Mind

Fasting is the process of abstaining from food for a specific period of time for spiritual purposes. Though the definition of fasting is listed above, a summary of fasting is simply denying oneself while seeking a more intimate relationship with God. This puts an individual in a better position to hear from God and to draw closer to him. Primarily, fasting includes food; however, you may find something else that you think has a dominant role in your life such as crafting, video games, social media, and so on. Sacrificing these items, in addition to or in lieu of food, may be more appropriate as it may be a greater challenge for you to abstain from it. The concept is to use that additional time to focus on prayer and God's word. There is not necessarily a right or wrong way to fast as long as you have peace from God regarding your fast, giving your commitment to Him beforehand with specifics about your intentions. During my study and seeking peace from God about fasting, I've adopted several types of fasts.

**Daniel Fast ➤** It is referred to in scripture that Daniel either fasted or was on his usual diet in periods of 10 and then 21 days. For a time period of 10 or 21 days, you are only to eat fruit, vegetables, nuts, seeds, and foods produced from seeds. Be sure to restrain from sweeteners, leavened bread, and any types of processed food. Be sure to look at nutritional labels before indulging in what may appear appropriate. Water should be your only beverage. Though green tea and such drinks are good for you, water is the only option on the Daniel fast. Likewise, wheat is natural and could be an option though 100% wheat bread is NOT allowed being it is leavened bread. While fruit is permitted, you should avoid fruit stored in syrup or fruit juice (canned fruit, etc.).

**Daniel Principles** ➤ For some time of your choice, you are only to have fruit, vegetables, nuts, seeds, and foods produced from seeds. Be sure to restrain from sweeteners, leavened bread, and any types of processed food. Be sure to look at nutritional labels before indulging in what may appear to be appropriate. Water should be your only beverage. Though green tea and such drinks are good for you, water is the only option on the Daniel fast. Likewise, wheat is natural and could be an option though 100% wheat bread is NOT allowed being its leavened bread. While fruit is permitted, you should avoid fruit stored in syrup or fruit juice (canned fruit, etc.).

**Fruits & Vegetables** ➤ For any time period, you are only to have fruits and vegetables. Unlike the Daniel fast/principles, you may add on to your fruits and vegetables. This may include sprinkling sugar on strawberries or drizzling caramel on apples. This may consist of eating carrots with ranch, fruit from a can, or cheese on broccoli. These are just a few examples of applying add-ons to your fruits and vegetables. You are not bound to any beverage though alcohol and other drinks that may be harmful to you should be avoided.

**Fruit of the Spirit Fast** ➤ For nine days, you are only to have fruit. Unlike the Daniel fast/principles, vegetables, nuts, and seeds are not allowed on this fast. You may also add on to your fruit. This may include sprinkling sugar on strawberries or drizzling caramel on apples. Additionally, you can eat canned fruit or fruit stored in syrup. Tomatoes are also considered a fruit. You are not bound to any particular type of beverage though alcohol and other drinks that may be harmful to you should be avoided.

**No Meat** ➤ For any time period, abstain from eating any types of meat and meat flavoring (example: meat flavored spaghetti sauce, chicken and beef broths, etc.).

**No Bread** ➤ For any time period, abstain from eating bread, crackers, biscuits, rolls, or buns. This could also include French toast sticks and other breakfast pastries such as muffins; but as indicated above, be specific when you commit to Christ as the definition of bread can be challenging.

**Liquid Fast** ➤ For any period of time, abstain from all food. You may, however, juice fruits and vegetables or make fruit shakes/smoothies on this fast. Any beverage is accepted though alcohol should be avoided.

**No Sweets** ➤ For any time period, abstain from sweet sugary snacks, cakes, pies, sugar, candy and candy bars, and anything, including beverages that have added sugar. Be sure to check nutritional labels during this fast. Natural glucose or sugar (pineapples, bananas, etc.) is allowed.

**Water Fast** ➤ For any period of time, abstain from everything except water. Occasionally, I will include a mint or cough drop with the water.

---

As a few cautionary procedures as you begin to fast, I would encourage you, first, to understand what is allowed on your fast before starting a fast. Next, you will want to ensure you have the appropriate foods accessible. Knowing your body and training it to be ready for such fasts is essential. For example, if you have not committed to fasting before, your first fast should not be 40-day water fast. While this example may be extreme, do not lose sight of the significance. At the same time, you should be challenged while fasting. Be wise in selecting your fasts. While the devotional will ask you to follow along with a specific fast for that month, feel free to choose one of the fasts above or develop your own if you feel uncomfortable following along with the specific fast.

As we begin, I want you to be mindful that *fasting* and *dieting* are not the same thing. While you may lose weight while fasting, weight loss is not – and should not – be the focus. Developing a regular healthy diet – which should be defined by the individual and their health care provider – can help you transition easier whenever a fast comes up.

A few other tips include easing in and out of your fast. Do not alter your eating habits immediately. Begin preparing your body to enter and exit the fast versus immediately starting and stopping your fast – *the flip the switch method*. Also, you should prepare your food beforehand. This includes acquiring and preparing. Finally, as stated earlier, know your body. Consult with a healthcare physician before altering your eating regime. This fasting series will be a challenge, but do not overdo it. Be specific when you give your commitment to God regarding your fast. If you commit your fast to Him, be sure to seek peace from God should you decide to alter it. As a reminder, neither author is, nor claim to be, medical professionals or mental health professionals. Therefore, be sure to consult with your healthcare provider before altering diet regimes or with a mental health professional if you are experiencing mental health challenges. God Bless you as you begin your journey.

# MONTH 1

## Laying the Foundation

*The Business of the Mind*

*I woke up one day, looked in the mirror, and didn't like what I saw.* Well, it didn't happen that way for me. For me, it all happened over time. For me, it was a series of events that would change me from the inside out.

After putting little to no pressure on my right leg for three months after ankle surgery, pancakes, pain medicine, and poor decisions helped me add a double-digit number in pounds to my frame that already suffered from carrying weight over the Body Mass Index for my height. I tried to eat a little better once I started walking to, mentally, help my connective tissues heal. I found myself making a few good decisions, but I would follow those good decisions up with several bad decisions. I struggled with consistency.

Six months after surgery, which was three months post-putting pressure on my ankle (walking) and wanting to eat better but continuing to fail, I started thinking about several events in my life where I spent a lot of time encouraging and seeing potential in others, all the while not knowing that I was losing myself. The Bible commands us to "love our neighbor as we love ourselves," but how can we love others if we have a negative self-concept of ourselves. At this point, I realized I needed a little encouragement. I needed investing in, and I needed to love myself enough to do just that.

During that time, something was placed on my mind. It was to go on a fast, the Daniel Fast, to be specific. To this point, the only thing I knew about the Daniel Fast was that it lasted 21 days! Well, I had not really fasted since my days in college. Could I manage three weeks of fasting? I eventually learned more information on the Daniel Fast but still knew very little. However, I decided to obey what I felt and embark on this fast.

Once the fast started, I began to investigate what I could eat and what I could not eat. I will admit. I made a great mistake by waiting to do this. I really should have studied the scriptures first and conducted additional research before beginning this fast. The fast was more difficult because I did not do the extra studying beforehand. I fasted the first two days, and I was faithful to the principles. However, day three found me mentally exhausted, frustrated, and confused. I began to pray, and toward the end of the day, I received peace to discontinue the Daniel Fast. However, I did commit to fasting for 21 days, so I did not want to conclude it altogether. Part of me receiving peace was continuing the fast, but I would continue it with different principles.

After completing this fast and going into the months to follow, I thought of some reasons why I suffered from low self-esteem, why I had so many insecurities, and why I felt inferior in specific environments. To help address those issues, I thought it was important that I tend to *The Business of the Mind* by developing a strong mind; and to do that successfully, I would need to develop a high level of *discipline* and *consistency*.

This month, I encourage you to model the fasting routine that laid the foundation for me to tend to *The Business of the Mind*. There are three foundational scriptures for this journey that we will examine over three consecutive weeks in our first month.

# Week 1 | Days 1-7

**Fast:** No Meat

**Devotion:** 2 Timothy 1:7 (Foundational Scripture 1 of 3)

"For God has not given us a spirit of fear, but of power, love, and of a sound mind."

---

This text deals with four things: the spirit of fear, power, love, and a sound mind.

A lot of decisions are made based on fear. It may be the fear of failure, or the fear of what others may think, say, or feel. However, that fear is not of God. God did not give us that fear. Instead, Paul says that God gave us three other spirits: the spirit of power, love, and a sound mind.

The concept of power is indicative of strength. Rikki Rogers said, "Strength doesn't come from what you can do. It comes from overcoming the things you once thought you [could not do]."

Love is a central theme in scripture ranging from "God is Love" in 1 John 1:4 and "God is our refuge and Strength" in Psalm 46. When we think of love, we will typically think of the heart. When we think of strength, we may typically think of muscles. The heart is one of the strongest muscles in the human body, so it is no surprise that it takes strength sometimes to love. Vincent Van Gogh said, "Love many things, for therein lies the true strength, and whosoever loves much performs much and can accomplish much, and what is done in love is done well."

A sound mind in the text, and in general, translates directly to self-discipline. Part of the mind's business is for it to become strong. A *strong mind* is disciplined. Through discipline (and consistency), one can truly work toward and achieve a *strong mind*. It takes both, however. It takes consistency in your approach to life, consistency in your approach to each day, consistency to evaluate each independent decision you will make. One with a strong mind moves to make decisions based on principles, values, and goals rather than convenience and emotions. Once a strong mind has been (or is being) developed, then the process of accomplishing any task you want to accomplish can begin.

This week, focus each day on 2 Timothy 1:7. Psalm 119:11 declares, "I have hidden Your word in my heart…". Over these next seven days, commit this scripture to memory and its location in the Bible; hide it in your heart, and remember that you have victory over fear. This is victory over the fear of failure, the victory over the fear of being inadequate, and the fear of being yourself. As we prepare for this month, I leave you, on the next page, with a quote from Marian Wright Edelman.

"Our deepest fear is not that we are inadequate. Our deepest fear is that we are powerful beyond measure. It is our light, not our darkness that most frightens us. We ask ourselves. Who am I to be brilliant, gorgeous, talented, fabulous? Actually, Who are you not to be? You are a child of God. And your playing small does not serve the world. Nothing is enlightening about shrinking so that other people won't feel insecure around you. We were all meant to shine as children do. We were born to make manifest the glory of God that is within us. And it is not just in some of us. It is in all of us. So, as we let our own light shine, we unconsciously give others permission to do the same. As we are liberated from our own fears, our presence automatically liberates others."

# Week 2 | Days 8-14

**Fast:** No fried foods

**Devotion:** Romans 12:2 (foundational scripture 2 of 3)

"Do not be conformed to this world but be ye transformed by the renewing of your mind."

---

The battle between conforming and transforming should be a daily thought. While our flesh would like us to conform, that is, "to the patterns and customs of this world," our *strong mind* (our disciplined mind) tells us to be transformed, "transformed by the way we think." Think about what you think about! What do most of your thoughts amount to? Are your thoughts consumed with negativity? Are your thoughts simply reflective of what other people think about? This can begin with merely deciding on lunch at work or participating in gossip. You can conform by eating convenient foods that everyone else is eating or by engaging in talk via speaking or listening. Or you can choose to be transformed by the way you think and live by the principles that guide you. One with a *strong mind* tends to make decisions based on principles, values, and goals rather than convenience and emotions.

This week, you may have decided to follow the fasting routine and alleviate fried foods from your diet. It takes a renewed mind to be disciplined to say "no" to those particular food items. However, by transforming the way you think, you can approach this endeavor with a strong mind (self-discipline). As you go on your day today, focus on your thoughts for the remainder of this week. What are your dominant thoughts throughout this week, either positive or negative? Record those thoughts throughout this week on the designated lines below.

Day 1 _____

_____

Day 2 _____

_____

Day 3 _____

_____

Day 4 _____

_____

Day 5 _____

_____

Day 6 _____

_____

Day 7 _____

_____

Now that you have an inventory of your thoughts, what *should* your thoughts be focused on? How do you become transformed by renewing your mind (or changed by the way you think)? Let us keep the consistency as we move into week three.

# Week 3 | Days 15-21

**Fast:** You may eat what you want, but only drink water as your beverage.

**Devotion:** Romans 8:5-6 (foundational scripture 3 of 3)

"For those who live according to the flesh set their minds on things of the flesh, but those who live according to the Spirit, set their minds on things of the Spirit."

---

Last week, you focused *on* your thoughts by writing down your dominant thoughts for the week, whether positive or negative. This week, you will *focus your thoughts*. This week's text gives us a choice. We can live according to our flesh or live according to the Spirit. We decide simply by what we set our minds on. Our flesh desires things of this world, which would be harmful to our souls. Things that would require us to conform. However, the Spirit gives life, and the text says that if we set our mind on things of the Spirit, we can live according to the Spirit. We can let the Spirit guide our lives. We can allow the Spirit to order our steps. I have a daily prayer, and a portion of it goes like this:

> Lord, I pray that You order my steps. Show me what to do and how to do it, dear Lord. Use me for Your glory. Help me not to be conformed to this world, to the patterns and customs, Lord. But help me to be transformed; transformed by the renewing of my mind. Transformed by the way I think. I pray for discipline and consistency. Consistency to allow my mind to remain focused on You,

## LAYING THE FOUNDATION

focused on the Spirit, and focused on Your Word. For we want to live according to the Spirit, and we want to be pleasing in Your sight, O, Lord.

As you enter into each day of this week, recite this prayer each day – or some variation of it. Even as you think of the anxieties this week may present, *focus your thoughts* on things of the Spirit. Record some of your fears, concerns, and frustrations that arise this week on the left side of the chart on the next page. On the right side, record *Spirit* thoughts, scriptures, and/or quotes that will help put a positive perspective to those anxieties, concerns, and frustrations.

## Focused Thoughts

| Anxieties, Concerns, & Frustrations | Spirit thoughts |
|---|---|
| Ex. I'm uneasy because I will be flying in an airplane for the first time. | Ex. Psalm 121:8 the LORD will watch over your coming and going both now and forevermore. |

## MONTH 2

# Fruit and Root

*The Business of the Mind*

We often see people in certain situations but give little thought about why they are in those situations. A few examples may include a lady who is disrespectful to her husband, a young man who is insubordinate on the job, or a parent who is overprotective of her children. We see those situations as the "fruit." There may be things to try and modify those behaviors, but those potential solutions may never really work. However, by looking at their situations a little deeper, we learn that it is not a *fruit* issue but a *root* issue – meaning a deeper cause for what is seen.

Similarly, we may see someone in a prosperous position, in a healthy relationship, or in good health. These are examples displaying positive fruit produced from a positive root.

While we can go deeper and acknowledge the need to begin the process of being healed from negative root behavior, let's focus on the content of one of our foundational scriptures for a strong mind that tells us "…those who live according to the Spirit set their minds on things of the Spirit."

In relationship to *fruit* and *root*, we take this month to study the *fruit of the Spirit*. The term Fruit of the Spirit tells us directly that the *root is the Spirit*. Therefore, the nine attributes (or qualities) explained in the text (the fruit) directly correlate with the source they are produced from, which is the Spirit.

As you go through this month, dedicate nine consecutive days to set your mind on things of the Spirit: the fruit of the Spirit. Each day, focus on one textual fruit. As I went through this study, I engaged in a nine-day fast where I only ate fruit. This was one of the most challenging fasts I have done but one of the most rewarding as well. This is a fantastic opportunity to begin renewing your mind. So, I challenge you to partake in the fruit of the Spirit fast (refer to page x) as you read and study this text.

**²²But the fruit of the Spirit is love, joy, peace, patience, kindness, goodness, faithfulness, ²³gentleness, self-control; against such things there is no law."**

Galatians 5:22-23 ESV

# Month 2 | Day 1

**Fast:** Fruit only and any beverage (no alcohol)
*Refer to Fruit of the Spirit fast*
**Devotion:** Galatians 5:22 "But the fruit of the Spirt is love…"

---

Love is the first of the nine *fruit of the Spirit* mentioned in Galatians 5:22-23. Love is a central theme in the Bible, and there are some great verses and stories in the Bible that center around love. Perhaps, the most incredible love story of all can be found in the third chapter of John, where it states, "For God so loved the world that he gave his only begotten son, that whosoever believeth in him shall not perish, but have everlasting life. For God sent his Son into the world not to condemn the world, but that the world through him might be saved" (John 3:16-17, NKJV).

Focus your thoughts today on *love*. Also, realize that it is up to us to love, not to condemn. As you go through this day focusing your thoughts on love, review the scriptures referenced on the next page and how they relate to verses 16 and 17 in the 3rd chapter of John. I encourage you to read these scriptures at least 3 to 5 times throughout this day. I even encourage you to begin praying the scriptures. These actions will help you keep your thoughts focused on *love:* God's love for us, our love for God, and our love towards one another.

## 1 John 4:8

But anyone who does not love does not know God, for **God is love**.

## 1 Corinthians 13:13

**Three things will last forever** – faith, hope, and love – and **the greatest of these is love**.

## Romans 12:9

Don't just pretend to love others. **Love them**....

## 1 Corinthians 13:4-7

[4]Love is patient and kind. Love is not jealous or boastful or proud [5]or rude. It does not demand its way. It is not irritable, and it keeps no record of being wronged. or rude. It does not demand its way. It is not irritable, and it keeps no record of being wronged. [6]It does not rejoice about injustice but rejoices whenever the truth wins out. [7]Love never gives up, never loses faith, is always hopeful, and endures through every circumstance.

## Matthew 22:37-39

[37]Jesus replied, "You must love the Lord your God with all your heart, all your soul, and all your mind. [38]This is the first and greatest commandment. [39]A second is equally important: 'Love your neighbor as yourself.'"

> **1 John 4:18-20**
>
> [18]Such love has no fear because perfect love expels all fear. If we are afraid, it is for fear of punishment, which shows that we have not fully experienced his perfect love. [19]We love each other because he loved us first. [20]If someone says, "I love God," but hates a fellow believer, that person is a liar; for if we don't love people we can see, how can we love God, whom we cannot see?

**Prayer:** Father, thank You for loving me. As I go on my day today, help me to obey Romans 12:9 and really love others rather than pretending to love them. Help me to know love and to show love because You are love, God, according to 1 John 4:8. For according to 1 Corinthians 13:4 and 5, we know that love is patient, kind, not jealous, not boastful, not prideful, or rude, so help me to be *patient* when I feel anxious, *kind* when I feel annoyed, *supportive* when I feel jealous, and *humble* and *polite* when I feel prideful or rude. Let Your love comfort me and let Your love stay on my mind today. In Jesus' name, Amen.

# Month 2 | Day 2

**Fast:** Fruit only and any beverage (no alcohol)
*Refer to Fruit of the Spirit fast*

**Devotion:** Galatians 5:22 "But the fruit of the Spirt is …joy…."

---

Joy is not to be confused with happiness, for happiness is circumstantial. Happiness is based on what happens to you. However, Joy refers to something internal. Joy is a filling rather than a feeling. Joy refers to a mindset established after a relationship with the Father is developed and cultivated. Joy does not mean that you are always upbeat and that nothing wrong ever happens to you, but Joy provides an attitude, mindset, and perspective that will allow you to be peaceful, pleasant, and pure throughout those times when things may be frustrating.

As you experience the pressures and anxieties as you go on this day, read the reference scriptures on the next page at least 3 to 5 times throughout this day to help keep your thoughts focused on joy; for the Joy of the Lord will be your strength. Even begin to pray these scriptures throughout the day.

## FRUIT AND ROOT

### Nehemiah 8:10 NLT

…Don't be dejected and sad, for **the joy of the Lord is your strength!**

### Psalm 30:5 NLT

For his anger lasts only a moment, but his favor lasts a lifetime! Weeping may last through the night, but **joy comes with the morning.**

### Isaiah 55:12 NLT

**You will live in joy** and peace. The mountains and hills will burst into song, and the trees of the field will clap their hands!

**Prayer:** Father, thank You for this day. Even as things may come across my mind today that would make me unhappy, I thank You that happiness is circumstantial, but Your Joy, Lord, no man can take from [me] according to John 16:22. And just as Jesus rose early one Sunday morning bringing Joy to the world, I know according to Psalm 30:5 that weeping may last through the night, but Joy comes with the morning. So, as I go on my day today, help me to experience Your Joy; for according to Nehemiah 8:10, the Joy of the Lord is my strength; and I *will* live in Joy according to Isaiah 55:12. Let Your Joy consume me today and let the Joy of the Lord stay on my mind today. In Jesus' name, Amen.

## Month 2 | Day 3

**Fast:** Fruit only and any beverage (no alcohol)
*Refer to Fruit of the Spirit fast*
**Devotion:** Galatians 5:22 "But the fruit of the Spirt is ...peace...."

---

Peace is knowing that God is in control no matter what happens in your life. A great story that highlights this principle comes from Jeremiah 29:4-14. While the Israelites were in bondage, God used Jeremiah to speak to them to say that I will bring you (your people) from this place one day in the distant future. Still, while you are here, your prosperity and peace depend on the prosperity and peace of this place you are in. So, instead of waiting until I bring you out of this place to find peace, find peace in the current situation and current environment you are in now. "For I know the thoughts (or plans) that I think toward (or have for) you, says the LORD, thoughts of peace and not of evil, to give you a future and a hope." (Jeremiah 29:11)

As you think of the situations you are in now, find ways to make the best of them. There may be greener pastures in the future but live in the present. Find peace in your current place, in your current environment, and in your current situations. Trust God. Read Jeremiah 29: 4-14 and draw a comparison between you and the Israelites. As you go throughout today, read the scriptures on the next page at least three times throughout this day. This will help you keep your thoughts focused on *peace*.

## FRUIT AND ROOT

### Philippians 4:6-7

⁶Don't worry about anything; instead, pray about everything. Tell God what you need and thank him for all he has done. ⁷ Then, **you will experience God's peace, which exceeds anything we can understand**. His peace will guard your hearts and minds as you live in Christ Jesus.

### Isaiah 55:12 NLT

**You will live in joy and peace**.
The mountains and hills will burst into song,
And the trees of the field will clap their hands!

### Isaiah 26:3 NKJV

**You will keep him in perfect peace**, Whose mind stays on You, Because he trusts in You.

### John 14:27 NLT

I am leaving you with a gift—peace of mind and heart. And the peace I give is a gift the world cannot provide. So don't be troubled or afraid.

### Romans 12:18

As much as it depends on you, possible, live peaceably with all men.

**Prayer:** Father, thank You for this day. As I begin my day, help me oh, Lord, to find peace in my current place, in my current environment, and in my everyday situations. As much as it depends on me, Lord, help me to live peaceably with everyone according to Romans 12:18. Help me not to be troubled or afraid, for I know according to John 14:27, that I have the gift of peace of mind. Help me to keep my mind stayed on you, according to Isaiah 26:3, so that I can remain in Your perfect peace. Let Your peace rest upon me today. In Jesus' name, Amen.

## Month 2 | Day 4

**Fast:** Fruit only and any beverage (no alcohol)
*Refer to Fruit of the Spirit fast*
**Devotion:** Galatians 5:22 "But the fruit of the Spirt is ...patience...."

---

Patience is not just about waiting, but rather the temperament and preparation while you're waiting. Patience is about emotional control. God promised Abram that he would have an heir. He began to get older, as did his wife, but they had no children. Abram soon agreed with his wife to sleep with her servant to produce a child. Abram should have waited with patience for his heir from God. God promised Abram something, but Abram got discouraged when he didn't see any results. He should have stayed with patience and trusted God, but instead, he slept with Hagar and she bore Ishmael. This later became a problem when his wife bore Isaac, the son God promised.

Conversely, Joseph did wait patiently – as you will read in month 10. God showed Joseph a vision in his youth that did not come to fruition until he was much older and had gone through many difficult times. Patience has a unique correlation with trust, and the actions taken while waiting will measure your trust.

As you go on this day, think about patience as you interact with people. Whether this is with a child, student, teacher, employee, employer, cashier, etc., think about the word patience and how you can be patient with this individual. Also, to keep your mind focused on thoughts of *patience*, read the scriptures on the next page and stay in the mind of *patience* today; patience in a spiritual and practical sense.

### Isaiah 40:31

But those who wait on the LORD Shall renew their strength; They shall mount up with wings like eagles, They shall run and not be weary, They shall walk and not faint.

### James 5:7

Therefore **be patient**, brethren, until the coming of the Lord. See how the farmer waits for the precious fruit of the earth, waiting patiently for it until it receives the early and latter rain.

### Galatians 6:9

So, **let's not get tired** of doing what is good. We will reap a harvest of blessings at just the right time **if we don't give up**.

### Romans 5:3-5

³And not only that but we also glory in tribulations, knowing **that tribulation produces perseverance;** ⁴ **and perseverance, character**; and character, hope. ⁵ Now, hope does not disappoint because the love of God has been poured out in our hearts by the Holy Spirit who was given to us.

**Prayer:** Father, thank You for the opportunity to serve in the roles that You have allowed me to serve in. Even as I'm waiting, Lord, for certain things to happen for my good in these roles, help me to display the proper demeanor in my waiting. Help me not to get tired of doing what is good. For I know if I do not give up, according to

Galatians 6:9, I will reap a harvest of blessings at just the right time. So, as I am in tribulation now, Lord, let me remember that tribulation produces perseverance, and perseverance character, and character hope according to Romans 5:3 and 4; and I put my hope in You according to Psalm 33:20. Hope that my strength can even be renewed. So, I will exercise Isaiah 40:31 and wait on You. In Your son Jesus' name. Amen.

# Month 2 | Day 5

**Fast:** Fruit only and any beverage (no alcohol)
*Refer to Fruit of the Spirit fast*
**Devotion:** Galatians 5:22 "But the fruit of the Spirt is
…kindness…."

---

One of the best ways to feel good about yourself is to show kindness to someone else. It only takes a simple gesture to show kindness to someone. Kindness is an act of humility, simply showing that you care for someone else. Think of a moment when you felt discouraged but kept it to yourself. How would you have thought if a random stranger or close friend came up and gave you a simple *pat on the back* or word of encouragement, not even knowing you needed it. Imagine struggling in line at a store, and the person in front of you allows you to go ahead of them. Wouldn't it be nice to treat yourself to dinner one night to find out someone across the restaurant has taken care of your ticket? These are just a few examples of showing kindness to someone else. And, when we show kindness, it should not be to receive anything in return or to boast about what we have done. We should show kindness for the sake of kindness. If the *root* is the Spirit and the Spirit is inside us, our *fruit* of kindness should *grow* naturally.

As you go throughout this day, read the scriptures on the next page and pray the scriptures at least three times throughout this day. This will help you keep your thoughts focused on *kindness*.

### 2 Samuel 9:1 NKJV

Now David said, "Is there still anyone who is left of the house of Saul that **I may show him kindness** for Jonathan's sake?

### Colossians 3:12 NLT

Since God chose you to be the holy people he loves, you must **clothe yourselves with** tenderhearted mercy, **kindness**, humility, gentleness, and patience.

**Prayer:** Father, thank You for Your kindness. It is Your kindness that helps keep me encouraged. Since I am a representation of You, Lord, and You chose me to be a holy people according to Colossians 3:12, I will clothe myself with kindness; even as David showed Your kindness to Mephibosheth in 2 Samuel 9, help me not only show kindness to those I come in contact with today, but help me to show Your kindness to those that may be connected to those who have showed kindness to me. I thank You for trusting me, and I pray that You continue to be with me. In Jesus' name. Amen.

# Month 2 | Day 6

**Fast: Fast:** Fruit only and any beverage (no alcohol)
*Refer to Fruit of the Spirit fast*

**Devotion:** Galatians 5:22 "But the fruit of the Spirt is

…goodness…"

---

Thoughts related to the word *good* include favorable, desirable, or positive. When we think of the holiday season, flavorful food around family is one thought. When we think of vacations, guilt-free relaxation in relaxing environments is another form. Goodness, however, is a characteristic of the Spirit of God. Goodness should also be one of our best qualities as a person. We all have a ministry within us. Showing goodness to others is a great way to serve them. We can show goodness to others in a variety of ways. Some are: Smiling at others, speaking in a friendly way to others, whether friends or strangers, congratulating others for their accomplishments, and encouraging others. There are several ways to show goodness to others. Furthermore, showing goodness to others takes your mind off of yourself. Often, we spend too much time focused on our own goals and agendas that we put off being good to others. Take this time to think of yourself less and concentrate on opportunities to display goodness to someone else.

### Galatians 6:10 NKJV

**Therefore**, as we have the opportunity, **let us do good to all,** especially to those who are of the household of faith.

### Psalm 23:6 NKJV

**Surely goodness and mercy shall follow me** All the days of my life; And I will dwell[a] in the house of the LORD Forever.

### Psalm 31:19

Oh, **how abundant is your goodness**, which you have stored up for those who fear you and worked for those who take refuge in you, in the sight of the children of humanity!

**Prayer:** Heavenly Father, I thank You for Your goodness. You have been better to me than I deserve. Father, because You are good to me, I desire Your strength to show goodness to others. In 1 Corinthians chapter 6 and verse 19, Your word says that my body is the temple of the Holy Spirit which I have from God. Lord, You live in me and that is the only way I can possess goodness. As it is written in Galatians chapter 6 and verse 10, help me to take advantage of opportunities to do good to all. In Jesus' name, I pray. Amen.

# Month 2 | Day 7

**Fast:** Fruit only and any beverage (no alcohol)
*Refer to Fruit of the Spirit fast*

**Devotion:** Galatians 5:22 "But the fruit of the Spirt is ...faithfulness...."

---

As humanity became distant from God, evil and more violent, God decided to rid the Earth of humans. However, He wanted to save Noah and his family. The Creator of all humanity spoke to Noah and commanded him to build an ark that would keep him, his family, as well as clean and unclean animals from the flood that was coming. Noah was given specific directions on how the ark was designed and built. By faith, Noah built the ark, which kept his family alive. Hebrews 11:1 says, "Now faith is the assurance of things hoped for, the conviction of things not seen." Noah had never built an ark before. Nor had he experienced a flood before. He navigated this test only through faith.

Throughout life, we will experience unexplainable circumstances. However, when we trust God and have faith in Him, we will survive whatever we face, just as Noah did. Also, Noah's faith did not only help him, but he was also able to bless his family by exercising faith and remaining faithful to what he needed to do.

As you consider the word faith today, set aside specific times to refer back to the scriptures to follow which focuses on faith. Read these scriptures at least five times throughout this day. This will help you keep your thoughts focused.

# FRUIT AND ROOT

### Hebrews 11:1-7 NKJV

¹Now faith is the [a]substance of things hoped for, the [b]evidence of things not seen. ² For by it, the elders obtained a good testimony. ³ By faith we understand that the [c]worlds were framed by the word of God so that the things which are seen were not made of visible things. ⁴ By faith, Abel offered God a more excellent sacrifice than Cain, through which he obtained witness that he was righteous, God testifying of his gifts; and through it, he being dead still speaks. ⁵ By faith Enoch was taken away so that he did not see death, "and was not found, because God had taken him"; for before he was taken, he had this testimony, that he pleased God. ⁶ But without faith it is impossible to please Him, for he who comes to God must believe that He is and that He is a rewarder of those who diligently seek Him. ⁷By faith Noah, being divinely warned of things not yet seen, moved with godly fear, prepared an ark for the saving of his household, by which he condemned the world and became heir of the righteousness which is according to faith.

### Hebrews 11:6 NKJV

But **without faith, it is impossible to please Him**, for he who comes to God must believe that He is and that He is a rewarder of those who diligently seek Him.

### 2 Corinthians 5:7

For we **walk by faith**, not by sight.

## THE BUSINESS OF THE MIND

> **Matthew 9:22**
>
> But Jesus turned around, and when He saw her, He said, "Be of good cheer, daughter; **your faith has made you well**." And the woman was made well from that hour.

**Prayer:** Father, I want to thank You for always showing faithfulness to me. You have never let me down; You are always there no matter what. Heavenly Father, I also thank You for Your Spirit. It is Your Spirit residing in me that enables me to display faithfulness to You. According to Hebrews 11:6, I must possess faith in order to please You. Thank You, Father, for strengthening my faith so I can walk in faithfulness. In Jesus' name, Amen.

# Month 2 | Day 8

**Fast:** Fruit only and any beverage (no alcohol)
*Refer to Fruit of the Spirit fast*

**Devotion:** Galatians 5:22-23 "But the fruit of the Spirt is …gentleness…."

---

Often gifts and talents such as singing, playing instruments, and orating are seen as exciting and valuable. Such talents like those above are recognized by many. Such actions get our attention. They also often bring fame. However, gentleness, or meekness, should be the most critical characteristic. Gentleness is a gift that can and should influence our society most positively. In a world full of racial and social prejudices, gentleness should be welcomed and embraced. Although gentleness is a fruit of the Spirit that is not always easy to model, it should never be obsolete in the kingdom of God. As long as the Spirit of God is alive, gentleness will never cease, and we should be intentional about making gentleness an everyday action. Allow God's Spirit to root you in gentleness. This may mean displaying gentleness to the angriest person you meet. This may include smiling at the stranger who seems to be having a bad day. Gentleness is an action, and there are numerous ways to be gentle. In the Kingdom of God, everyone will not be famous or wealthy; However, we can, with God's help, live in gentleness through the Holy Spirit. Gentleness is necessary. Gentleness should be named among those who are believers.

Read the scriptures on the next page at least five times throughout this day. This will help you keep your thoughts focused.

# FRUIT AND ROOT

### Philippians 4:5 NKJV

**Let your gentleness** be known to all men. The Lord is at hand.

### Galatians 6:1 NLT

Dear brothers and sisters, if another believer is overcome by some sin, **you who are godly should gently and humbly help** that person back onto the right path. And be careful not to fall into the same temptation yourself.

### Proverbs 15:1 NLT

**A gentle answer deflects anger**, but harsh words make tempers flare.

### 1 Corinthians 4:13 NLT

"We **appeal gently** when evil things are said about us.

**Prayer:** Lord, thank You for Your kindness and gentleness towards me. I also thank You for the mind and will to show gentleness to others according to Philippians 4:5. Oftentimes, Father, I was not deserving of Your gentleness. However, You are a forgiving God and I agree with Your words in Galatians chapter 6 and verse 1 that instructs me to restore the person fallen in sin gently and humbly helping them get back on the right path. Father, As I continue to serve You, help me to remember Your gentleness for me. In Jesus' name. Amen.

# Month 2 | Day 9

**Fast:** Fruit only and any beverage (no alcohol)
*Refer to Fruit of the Spirit fast*

**Devotion:** Galatians 5:22-23 "But the fruit of the Spirt is …and self-control.…"

---

The world of sports is a significant part of our society. Athletes are challenged mentally and physically. They learn the importance of individual toughness as well as teamwork. Whether the athlete participates in baseball, basketball, football, gymnastics, or cheerleading, they must have a life of self-control. Self-control for an athlete means multiple things. It means daily practice for hours in their field, cardio, weightlifting, developing a particular technique, collaborating with teammates, eating the proper diet, and implementing the necessary rest. For an athlete, it's more than showing up for the competition or game. All of the hard work, dedication, and discipline put into the particular field prepares them for competition.

As the athlete displays self-control and benefits in physical fitness, the believer has the responsibility and the right to practice self-control in life. Although challenging, it is possible, with the help of the Holy Spirit, to live a life of self-control. You will read about those who practiced this necessary characteristic throughout the Bible. For example, Daniel displayed self-control through his fasting. Daniel 10:3 says, "I ate no pleasant food, no meat or wine came into my mouth, nor did I anoint myself at all, till three whole weeks were fulfilled."

## FRUIT AND ROOT

Notice, Daniel did eat; however, he ate none of his favorite foods that were pleasing to him. Nor did he eat meat or drink wine for three weeks. Daniel practiced self-control. So can you! An additional person showing self-control in the Bible is Joseph. In Genesis 39, the Bible tells how Potiphar's wife tried to seduce Joseph sexually. It was the integrity and self-control of Joseph that enabled him to resist the temptation. Throughout life's journey, you will encounter various situations that will require self-control. Remember, the root of self-control and all of the fruit is the Spirit of the living God.

Galatians 5:22-23 declares, "But the fruit of the Spirit is love, joy, peace, patience, kindness, goodness, faithfulness, gentleness, self-control. Against such things, there is no law."

The scriptures below can help keep your thoughts focused. Read these scriptures at least five times throughout this day.

### 2 Timothy 1:7 (ESV)
For God gave us a spirit not of fear but of power and love and self-control.

### Proverbs 16:32 ESV
Whoever is slow to anger is better than the mighty, and he who rules his spirit than he who takes a city.

### Proverbs 25:28 ESV
A man without self-control is like a city broken into and left without walls.

### 1 Peter 4:7 ESV

The end of all things is at hand; therefore be self-controlled and sober-minded for the sake of your prayers.

### 1 Corinthians 10:13 ESV

No temptation has overtaken you that is not common to man. God is faithful, and he will not let you be tempted beyond your ability, but with the temptation, he will also provide the way of escape, that you may be able to endure it.

**Prayer:** Heavenly Father, I love You and thank You for who You are and all You do. Lord, I thank You for Your Spirit that enables me to be what You would have me to be. I cannot live a life of self-control without You. Father, help me to continue to display self-control, even in my weakest moments. According to Philippians 4:13, I can do it. Also, Lord, thank You for the Spirit of self-control in every area of my life. Although this may be difficult, Your Spirit makes this possible. In Jesus' name. Amen.

# MONTH 3

## On These Things

*The Business of the Mind*

What are you thinking about right now? Is your mind wandering as you read this devotional? Are you currently thinking: How will I do "this"? When will *it* happen? Why did they do that to me? Where will I end up? These are a few questions that possibly cross our minds daily. A good friend of mine, who is now in our Savior's presence, once prayed this prayer: "Lord, change my mind before my mind changes me!" It is imperative, as believers, that our minds be sane, sound, and sanctified.

Philippians 4:8 provides us with a blueprint on what to focus our minds on. The Apostle Paul writes, "Finally, brothers, whatever is true, whatever is honorable, whatever is just, whatever is pure, whatever is lovely, whatever is commendable, if there is any excellence, if there is anything worthy of praise, think about these things."

Building upon the work you completed in months one and two, this scripture text will be the focus of month three as we spend six days diving deeper into each individual "whatsoever statement."

# Month 3 | Day 1

**Fast:** No sweets – Water as only drink
*Abstain from sugary snacks, cakes, pies, sugar, candy, candy bars, and anything, including beverages, with added sugar. Natural glucose or sugar (pineapples, bananas, etc.) is allowed.*

**Devotion:** Philippians 4:8 "Finally, brothers, whatever is true, …"

---

Merriam-Webster defines "fact" as having actual existence or a natural occurrence. For example, you may be presently facing a trial. It is occurring at this very moment. However, when we focus on things that are true, the truth is, no matter where you are in life, "you are more than a conqueror," as stated in the book of Romans, chapter 8 and verse 37 (KJV).

Here are more true things to think about:

**Philippians 4:13 KJV** "I can do all things through Christ, which strengtheneths me."

*Fact:* I have failed.

*Truth:* I can do all things through Christ.

**Isaiah 53:5 KJV** "But he was wounded for our transgressions, he was bruised for our iniquities: the chastisement of our peace was upon him, and with his stripes, we are healed."

*Fact:* I am ill.

*Truth:* When Christ died on the cross, I became healed.

**Deuteronomy 28:13 KJV** "And the Lord shall make thee the head, and not the tail, and thou shalt be above only, and thou shalt not be beneath; if that thou hearken unto the commandments of the Lord thy God, which I command thee this day, to observe and to do them:"

*Fact:* I have a low self-image.

*Truth:* In Christ, I am the head. I am above.

**\*\*\*Your turn:** Below and on the next page, there is a fact for you; however, this is also an opportunity to open your truth!

**2 Timothy 1:7 KJ** "For God hath not given us the spirit of fear (timidity); but of power, and of love, and of a sound mind."

*Fact:* I am at times fearful/timid

*Truth:* _____

_____

**Proverbs 10:4 ESV** "A slack (lazy) hand causes poverty, but the hand of the diligent makes rich."

*Fact:* I am often lazy

*Truth:* _____

_____

## THE BUSINESS OF THE MIND

**2 Corinthians 12:9-10 ESV** "But he said to me, "My grace is sufficient for you, for my power is made perfect in weakness." Therefore, I will boast all the more gladly of my weaknesses so that the power of Christ may rest upon me. For the sake of Christ, then, I am content with weaknesses, insults, hardships, persecutions, and calamities. For when I am weak, then I am strong."

*Fact:* I am weak

*Truth:* _____

_____

**Galatians 5:16-24 ESV** "But I say, walk by the Spirit, and you will not gratify the desires of the flesh. For the desires of the flesh are against the Spirit, and the desires of the Spirit are against the flesh, for these are opposed to each other to keep you from doing the things you want to do. But if you are led by the Spirit, you are not under the law. Now the works of the flesh are evident: sexual immorality, impurity, sensuality, idolatry, sorcery, enmity, strife, jealousy, fits of anger, rivalries, dissensions, divisions, envy, drunkenness, orgies, and things like these. As I warned you before, I warn you that those who do such things will not inherit the kingdom of God. But the fruit of the Spirit is love, joy, peace, patience, kindness, goodness, faithfulness, gentleness, self-control; against such things, there is no law. And those who belong to Christ Jesus have crucified the flesh with its passions and desires."

*Fact:* I struggle with my flesh

*Truth:* _____

_____

# Month 3 | Day 2

**Fast:** No sweets – Water as only drink
*Abstain from sugary snacks, cakes, pies, sugar, candy, candy bars, and anything, including beverages, with added sugar. Natural glucose or sugar (pineapples, bananas, etc.) is allowed.*

**Devotion:** Philippians 4:8 "Finally, brothers, whatever is …honorable, …"

---

Honorable is a word of distinction and nobility. It also means honesty. When you think of this word, what comes to mind? Anything and everything that reflects Christ Jesus. He is honorable; He is honest. For example, recognizing a soldier who died for their country against its foes is considered noble. That is what our Savior Jesus did. He died so you and I could live!

The Word of God tells us in Romans 5:6-8 (ESV), "For while we were still weak, at the right time Christ died for the ungodly. For one will scarcely die for a righteous person—though perhaps for a good person one would dare even to die— but God shows his love for us in that while we were still sinners, Christ died for us." This is an honorable thing!

In the Scripture, honorable is a Greek word meaning whatever becomes you as a man/woman, a citizen, and a believer (Adam Clarke Commentary).

Honor and Honesty focuses on three main areas: our Humanity (becoming a man/woman), our Citizenship/Community, and our lives as Believers. Focus on the scripture reading on the next page, pen how God empowers you to be honorable in each area; and begin good thinking by letting God's Word penetrate your mind.

## Humanity (As a man/woman)

**Scripture Reading:** Psalm 139:13-14 (ESV), "For you formed my inward parts; you knitted me together in my mother's womb. I praise you, for I am fearfully and wonderfully made. Wonderful are your works; my soul knows it very well." - *As a man/woman, God made me in His image. God's works are beautiful!*

**Scripture Reading:** Genesis 1:26, 27 (ESV), "Then God said, "Let us make man in our image, after our likeness. And let them have dominion over the fish of the sea and the birds of the heavens and the livestock and all the earth and over every creeping thing that creeps on the earth. So, God created man in his image, in the image of God he created him; male and female he created them."

**Prayer:** Lord, I thank You that I am created in Your image, and You have given me authority over all the Earth. And while I am a man/woman, I need Your strength in my humanness. In Jesus' name. Amen.

**Activity:** God's word helps me honor Him in my humanity by _____

_____

_____

_____

_____

_____

THE BUSINESS OF THE MIND

## As a citizen

**Scripture Reading:** Matthew 17:27 (ESV), "However, not to give offense to them, go to the sea and cast a hook and take the first fish that comes up, and when you open its mouth, you will find a shekel. Take that and give it to them for yourself and me." - *As a citizen, we should exercise responsibility just as Jesus did in paying His taxes.*

**Prayer:** Lord, I praise You for the blessing of citizenship. Because of You, I am blessed to enjoy the everyday freedoms of the city, county, and state of my choosing. Because I am an Ambassador of Christ, please give me the strength to be the citizen that represents You. In Jesus' name. Amen.

**Activity:** God's word helps me honor Him in my citizenship/community by _____
_____
_____
_____

## As a believer

**Scripture Reading:** Colossians 3:17 (ESV), "And whatever you do, in word or deed, do everything in the name of the Lord Jesus, giving thanks to God the Father through him." - *As a believer, we should glorify our Heavenly Father in all that we say and do.*

**Scripture Reading:** Colossians 3:13 (ESV), "And whatever you do, in word or deed, do everything in the name of the Lord Jesus, giving thanks to God the Father through him."

**Prayer:** Father, I thank You for giving Your only Son, Jesus, to die for me. I believe and confess that Jesus died and has risen from the dead. Lord, help me live a life, as a believer, that brings honor to Your name. In Jesus' name. Amen.

**Activity:** God's word helps me honor Him in being a believer by ___
_____
_____
_____

# Month 3 | Day 3

**Fast:** No sweets – Water as only drink
*\*Abstain from sugary snacks, cakes, pies, sugar, candy, candy bars, and anything, including beverages, with added sugar. Natural glucose or sugar (pineapples, bananas, etc.) is allowed.*

Devotion: Philippians 4:8 "Finally, brothers, whatever is …just …"

---

The *Life Application Concise New Testament Commentary* defines *Just* to mean *Right*. The commentary further states that *Just* also can be defined as "Thoughts and plans that meet God's standards of rightness. They are in keeping with the truth; they are righteous."

We all have our standards when it comes to material things. Some have a standard of a specific make and model car they drive. Some have a standard of their clothing brand, while others may have a personal standard of the neighborhood they choose to live in. Although natural standards vary, God requires a *Just* standard that is possible to attain depending on personal preference.

The Word of God says, "…whatever is just, or right…think on these things." Do you have plans for tomorrow? For next week? For the rest of the year? Planning our routine is a positive act. Our plans, however, must meet God's standard of rightness. Reading God's word will keep our thoughts Just. Continue to think about God's plan for your life.

## Personal plans

**Scripture Reading:** Jeremiah 29:11 (ESV), "For I know the plans I have for you, declares the Lord, plans for wholeness and not for evil, to give you a future and a hope."

**Scripture Reading:** 2 Corinthians 10:5 (ESV), "We destroy arguments and every lofty opinion raised against the knowledge of God and take every thought captive to obey Christ."

**Prayer:** Father, I thank You for living in my mind; my thoughts belong to You, and if there are any evil or unpleasant thoughts, thoughts that are not just in Your sight, I pray You remove those thoughts, oh Lord; and replace them with thoughts that align with Your standard. I trust You to keep my mind in perfect peace. In Jesus' name. Amen.

**Activity:** I will replace my negative thoughts of _____

_____

_____

_____

with positive, Christ-like thoughts of _____

_____

_____

_____

# Month 3 | Day 4

**Fast:** No sweets – Water as only drink
*\*Abstain from sugary snacks, cakes, pies, sugar, candy, candy bars, and anything, including beverages, with added sugar. Natural glucose or sugar (pineapples, bananas, etc.) is allowed.*

---

**Devotion:** Philippians 4:8 "Finally, brothers, whatever is …pure …"

---

Pure is a Greek word that means *chaste* or *clean*. As human beings born into sin, we did not need any assistance learning to think evilly. Our sinful nature prohibits clean thinking; However, it is pure thinking that we must continuously work toward.

Matthew 23:25 (GW) declares, "How horrible it will be for you, scribes and Pharisees! You hypocrites! You clean the outside of cups and dishes. But inside, they are full of greed and uncontrolled desires."

Would you eat your favorite meal on a dirty plate with last week's food on it? I would think not! As believers, we must steadfastly work on our inner cleanliness and focus not only on our outer appearance.

**Activity:** I have impure thoughts concerning _____

_____

_____

_____

I will allow God to change my impure thoughts and behaviors to pure thoughts and behaviors by _____

_____

_____

**Prayer:** Father, I am naturally a sinner with evil thoughts; I ask that You forgive me for any uncleanness in my life. Father, I ask that You make me pure in thought and deed. In Jesus' name. Amen.

# Month 3 | Day 5

**Fast:** No sweets – Water as only drink
*\*Abstain from sugary snacks, cakes, pies, sugar, candy, candy bars, and anything, including beverages, with added sugar. Natural glucose or sugar (pineapples, bananas, etc.) is allowed.*

**Devotion:** Philippians 4:8 "Finally, brothers, whatever is …lovely, …"

---

We must remember how much our heavenly father loves us! John 3:16 (KJV) says, "For God so loved the world, that he gave his only begotten Son, that whosoever believeth in him should not perish, but have everlasting life." As believers, we are called to love ourselves, love others as God loves us, and love moral beauty and spiritual beauty.

In Philippians 4:8, lovely means thoughts of great moral and spiritual beauty, not evil. (Life Application New Testament Commentary)

*Moral* - Merriam-Webster Dictionary defines Moral as relating to principles of right and wrong in behavior: ethical-moral judgments. We are responsible for developing morals that bring glory to God; also, as believers, we do not call evil good and good evil. Isaiah 5:20 (ESV) declares, "Woe to those who call evil good and good evil, who put darkness for light and light for darkness, who put bitter for sweet and sweet for bitter!"

*Spiritual* - Spirit or spirituality can have multiple meanings. A spirit can be demonic or Satanic. Also, a spirit can be divine from God. However, when God breathed His breath into man, He put His Spirit into man. Since we have God's spirit, He gives us the capability to think about lovely things.

## ON THESE THINGS

**Scripture Reading:** Genesis 2:7 (KJV), "And the LORD God formed man *of* the dust of the ground and breathed into his nostrils the breath of life, and man became a living soul."

**Activity:** As my thinking relates to my morals, I practice good morals in things such as _____

_____
_____
_____
_____
_____

As my thinking relates to God's spirit living in me, I can practice thinking lovely in areas such as _____

_____
_____
_____
_____
_____

**Prayer:** Father, as I intentionally think on lovely things, help me to be mindful of the morals that I practice as I exalt You in all I do. In Jesus' name. Amen.

# Month 3 | Day 6

**Fast:** No sweets – Water as only drink
*Abstain from sugary snacks, cakes, pies, sugar, candy, candy bars, and anything, including beverages, with added sugar. Natural glucose or sugar (pineapples, bananas, etc.) is allowed.*

**Devotion:** Philippians 4:8 "Finally, brothers, whatever is …commendable, …"

---

Commendable things are those which are of a good report as stated in the King James Version of Philippians chapter 4, verse 8. Commendable can also be interpreted as things well spoken of.

The Life Application New Testament Commentary defines commendable as admirable. Admirable things speak well of the thinker—thoughts that recommend, give confidence in, afford approval or praise, reveal positive and constructive thinking. I heard that a believer's views should be admirable, not embarrassing.

One of our foundational scriptures, Romans 12:2 (ESV), tells us, "Do not be conformed to this world, but be transformed by the renewal of your mind, that by testing you may discern what the will of God is, what is good and acceptable and perfect." When we transform our minds, we change our thinking. Once our thinking has changed, we alter what we say and behave.

Lastly, Philippians 4:8 concludes by saying, "If there is any excellence, if there is anything worthy of praise, think about these things."

Excellence is moral excellence, nothing of substandard quality. Worthy of praise is a phrase that may be restated as "anything that deserves the thinker's praise" or "anything that God deems praiseworthy." (Life Application New Testament Commentary).

**Prayer:** Lord, I thank You for Your unconditional love towards me. I ask You to forgive me for not only thinking in a way that does not please You. Please forgive me for any words or behavior that did not bring glory to Your name. Thank You, Lord, for giving me another opportunity to please You in my thinking, talking, and actions. In Jesus' name. Amen.

**Activity:** When my thoughts are heard by others, I will exalt God by

_____
_____
_____
_____
_____

When my behaviors are seen by others, I will exalt God by

_____
_____
_____
_____
_____

# MONTH 4

## Establishing Your Worth

*The Business of the Mind*

An essential element in taking care of the business of my mind for me was to answer the question, "Who am I?" Often, we look at titles, what we do, and what we possess to define us. However, we need to understand that our worth is in Christ Jesus. Additionally, the thoughts we possess significantly impact our current situations. Ideas may not necessarily put us in poverty or bring sickness to us, but they very well could. They also could help keep us in that state or bring us out of that state.

The Bible states in Proverbs 18:21 that "Life and Death are in the power of the tongue." Therefore, we have the power to speak life. We can speak life over our situations, and we can speak life over our circumstances. We have the power to speak life over those dead areas in our lives. Whatever we say, positively or negatively, gets planted into our subconscious mind; and whether we realize it or not, it begins to take effect. Bishop Tudor Bismark stated, "Whatever follows I am, begins looking for you." Joel Osteen has also taken this position and speaks adamantly of the power of I AM.

For me, I realized that I did not like public speaking. I think that stemmed from lacking self-confidence. I think I spoke low because I was not sure of myself or didn't feel what I had to say had any fundamental importance. Maybe I was embarrassed to give a speech because my voice was raspy and not deep like I thought it should be. Then, I realized that God made me a certain way for a particular purpose. If he wanted us all to be the same, he would have made us that way. Granted, there were some things I could reasonably change, but there were also some things that I needed to accept.

Throughout my 18-month journey tending to the business of my mind (working toward a strong mind), I realized that the mind serves as a catalyst and provides momentum for other areas to follow. So, I began to use positive "I am" statements and positive affirmations to help define who I was and address some of my insecurities. I also started looking through the Bible and standing on some of the scriptures that allow us to speak victory over our lives. The Bible says, "when you are weak, say that I am strong." I begin to tell myself that "I am strong, I am confident, I am secure, I am worthy." I also began to say to myself that "I am articulate." Those were areas I felt in my life were weak. I put together a script of "I am" statements and positive affirmations that I would read to myself daily.

During this time, I also discovered Dr. Wayne Dyer. Dr. Dyer has a YouTube video that talks about this very principle. It also teaches us how to meditate on those principles. During this month, I took 30 minutes each Monday morning and followed alone as Dr. Dyer explained and went through this process. Also, each night before bed, I would read several of the "I am" statements and positive affirmations to myself. As you begin this month, in addition to reading the devotional text, think of various "I am" statements or positive affirmations that you can speak to yourself daily during this month (and after this month if you choose to do so). I also challenge you to mediate to either Dr. Dyer's video or to some other soft instrumental music that allows you to spend 30 minutes in mediation setting the atmosphere each Monday morning of this month.

# Month 4 | Monday Mornings

**Fast:** I did not fast during this time

**Devotion:** Exodus 3 (emphasis on verse 14)

"And God said unto Moses, I AM THAT I AM: and he said, Thus shalt thou say unto the children of Israel, I AM hath sent me unto you."

---

While the emphasis of this month's devotion is on verse 14, a summary of Exodus 3 will provide some context for verse 14 of the text. In this chapter, an angel of the Lord appeared to Moses in a burning bush, but the bush was not consumed by the fire. This caught Moses' attention, so he turned to the bush. It is here, that the Lord spoke to Moses explaining how He has heard the cries of His people (Israel) who were captive in Egypt by Pharoah. God explains that He will send Moses to tell Pharoah to release them.

It is in verse 11 that we see why establishing your worth is important. God has already chosen Moses for this assignment. Yet, Moses shows in verse 11 how unsure he was of himself when he said, "Who am I, that I should go unto Pharaoh, and that I should bring forth the children of Israel out of Egypt?" God had already chosen Moses, appeared to him, and spoke the assignment to him. Yet, Moses wasn't sure of his worth. Nevertheless, God affirms Moses by letting him know that he would be with him.

In verse 13, Moses clearly knows who God is as he begins to practice the speech he would deliver to the Israelites saying "…The God of your fathers hath sent me unto you." Here is where we will

## ESTABLISHING YOUR WORTH

begin to focus on verse 14 of this text as Moses considers what his response would be to the Israelites if they ask, "What is his name?"

God goes on to tell Moses in verse 14 "…I AM THAT I AM…, Thus shalt thou say unto the children of Israel, I AM hath sent me unto you."

**Activity:** Meditate each Monday Morning for 20-30 minutes using positive affirmations and "I AM" statements over soft music. I used Dr. Wayne Dyer's "I AM THAT I AM….". Read each night before bed these "I AM" statements/positive affirmations.

I am _____

I am _____

I am _____

I am _____

I am _____

I am _____

I am _____

I am _____

I am _____

I am _____

## THE BUSINESS OF THE MIND

(Ex. 1) Nothing is against me. I am walking with God, poised in His presence. Secure and unafraid. (Ex. 2) My body is healthy, and my mind is brilliant. (Ex 3) I have clarity in my mind. (Ex 4) I always speak calmly and clearly.

# MONTH 5

## The Life and Journey

*The Business of the Mind*

Life, no doubt, is a journey! It comes with ups and downs, flips and flops, heartache and heartbreak, sadness and smiles, cries and laughter, hate and love, along with wins and losses. There are times when we do not know what to do, where to go, or what to say. That's life, and it's all a part of the journey.

Sometimes those various cycles of ups and downs, wins and losses have to do with other people's perceptions of us. Those cycles may sometimes have to do with being rejected and overlooked. We will examine this month the life of David and his journey to be king.

As you spend 16 days reading about the life and journey of David, spend time to work through the activities this month to really grasp the content presented in this month.

# Month 5 | Day 1

**Fast:** I did not fast during this month.

**Devotion:** 1 Samuel 16:7 (MSG), "God told Samuel "Looks aren't everything. Don't be impressed with his looks and stature. I've already eliminated him. God judges persons differently than humans do. Men and women look at the face; God looks into the heart."

**How Man Sees**

In verses 8-11 of 1 Samuel 16, Jesse presented seven of his sons to Samuel. At least some of them were tall and good-looking. However, God had previously given Samuel the order not to consider their outer appearance. Upon the sons entering and Samuel not seeing the "chosen one," he asks Jesse the questions: "Is this it? Are there no more sons?" And Jesse, David's father, replies, "Well, yes, there's the runt...."

According to Webster's Dictionary, Runt means "a person of small stature." For most people, the word runt is used negatively. It can signify insignificance, struggle, and being the underdog. There are times you and I have been viewed as the runt, the insignificant one, the underdog. The good news is that this is man's opinion and not God's truth about us. You are not a runt in the eyes of your heavenly father. You are righteous, you have been reborn, and you are radiant!

**Prayer:** Lord, I thank You for the natural family I have been born into; I thank You for my looks, my height, my weight, and all of my physical attributes. Whether man considers me essential or not; significant or not, attractive or not, You are my father, and I am made in Your image. Thank You, Lord, for this life journey! I know You are with me! In Jesus' name, I pray. Amen!

**Activity:** Think for a moment. Have you ever been told you were insignificant? What was said? Write those things down and reflect on them; **This is not to dwell on, but to denounce those words!**

_____

_____

## How God Sees

It is true, in 1 Samuel 16:7b, that "Men and women look at the face...". As people, we view what the eyes can see and assess its value as good or bad, attractive or unattractive. Our humanity considers success and failure with our eyes. For instance, when we see a big, brick, beautiful home, we assume the owners are *well-to-do* and are thriving. This is a fair assessment. However, what we cannot see about the residents of the lovely home is their heart. We cannot see their thoughts. We cannot see their soul. God is the viewer of the heart and knows the intentions of it. Therefore, those who may not look successful in the eyes of others, very well could be successful. The perspective of God transcends into their heart! You may have nice material things; you may not. The critical questions we must ask ourselves is "How is my heart", "What does it look like", and "What is it filled with".

The Hebrew word for heart is lēbāb, which means the mind's most interior organ (Strong's Talking Greek & Hebrew Dictionary). When

## THE BUSINESS OF THE MIND

was the last time you looked at someone's heart or mind? You cannot! Only God, the Father, can do that! He knows our thoughts; He knows what we will say before we speak! That is why it is essential to ask God to take inventory of our hearts. Because we want it to be pure!

**Prayer:** Heavenly Father, I thank You for accepting me as I am; I thank You for cleansing my heart, my mind, and my soul. I give my heart to You! As I embark on this life journey, please guard my heart against becoming hard. Thank You for a soft heart! In Jesus' name, I pray. Amen!

**Activity:** In 1 Samuel 16:1 (MSG), "God addressed Samuel: 'So, how long are you going to mope over Saul? You know I have rejected him as king over Israel. Fill your flask with anointing oil and get going. I am sending you to Jesse of Bethlehem. I've spotted the very king I want among his sons.'" The Lord found the king of Israel that He wanted! Just in case you did not know, you are important to God! He chooses you! Below, please answer the question for today's activity.

What God sees in us is far more important than what others see! How does GOD see you?

_____
_____
_____
_____
_____

# THE LIFE AND JOURNEY

(cont.) _____

_____
_____
_____
_____
_____
_____
_____
_____
_____
_____
_____
_____

Remember, in this Life Journey; we will be underestimated; we will be called "runt." We may even be considered as the last and the least to some. Nonetheless, remember that God sees our heart! He knows things about us that others cannot see! Throughout life, keep God first, despite how others view you.

# Month 5 | Day 2

**Fast:** I did not fast during this month.

**Devotion:** 1 Samuel 17:34-36, 50 (ESV) "[34] But David said to Saul, "Your servant used to keep sheep for his father. And when there came a lion, or a bear, and took a lamb from the flock, [35] I went after him and struck him and delivered it out of his mouth. And if he arose against me, I caught him by his beard and struck him and killed him. [36] Your servant has struck down both lions and bears, and this uncircumcised Philistine shall be like one of them, for he has defied the armies of the living God."
[50] So David prevailed over the Philistine with a sling and a stone, struck the Philistine, and killed him. There was no sword in the hand of David."

---

**A Time to Keep**

I have kept and cared for a few pets in my life. As a child, although not at the same time, my family had a cat and several puppies. As a parent, I gave one of my sons a dog; He was very young, and I assisted him with the dog, Boomer. But a watcher of sheep, the animal, I have never been! David, however, had the experience of keeping sheep for his father. Sheep, being weak and vulnerable little creatures, needed protecting. David guarded the sheep against the lions and bears. I believe the keeping of the sheep, an unpopular task in the eyes of many, prepared David for his journey of conquering more remarkable feats in his life! Zechariah 4:10a (MSG) says, "Does anyone dare despise this day of small beginnings?" Just as David performed the dirty job of keeping sheep, you may be a keeper of something not significant or widespread. You may have been given a task that seems lesser than the task given to someone who appears to be more qualified. It is ok! The "keeping of your sheep" is preparing you for something big! Whatever you do, "keep the sheep" with excellence; "keep your sheep" with courage; "keep your sheep" with diligence!

**Prayer:** Lord, I thank You for the opportunity to be a keeper. When discouragement comes, I know You are with me and will give me strength to keep what has been entrusted to me consistently. Father, I trust You to lead me, guide me, and protect me. In the name of Jesus. Amen.

**Activity:** In 1 Samuel 17, David leaves the sheep to take food to his brothers. Upon David's arrival, the brothers of David demand that he goes back to keeping the sheep. However, David wanted to know more about the battle. David also explains how he has killed a lion and a bear to protect the sheep. Our small victories lead us to big victories. *Below, write down the small victories you have experienced while doing small tasks.*

_____

_____

_____

_____

_____

_____

# Month 5 | Day 3

**Fast:** I did not fast during this month

**Devotion:** 1 Samuel 18:1-4 (ESV) "As soon as he had finished speaking to Saul, the soul of Jonathan was knit to the soul of David, and Jonathan loved him as his own soul. And Saul took him that day and would not let him return to his father's house. Then Jonathan made a covenant with David because he loved him as he loved himself. And Jonathan stripped himself of the robe that was on him and gave it to David, and his armor, and even his sword and his bow and his belt."

---

## A Faithful Friend

Do you love God? Of course! So do I! If it had not been for the Lord who was on our side, where would we be? He forgave us, saved us, and set us free! Who would not serve a God like that?! We are forever thankful to Him! Although the statements are accurate, we also need encouraging, faithful, upbeat friends. We need friends in our lives who will celebrate and protect us! Life is a journey, and we will need faithful people willing to give.

**Prayer:** Lord, I thank You for my friend(s). I know You have blessed me to have such people in my life. I ask that You continue to lead, protect, and provide for them. Father, I also thank You for giving me the strength to be the friend that my friends need. In Jesus' name. Amen.

**Activity:**

Friend Name _____

What qualities make him/her a friend?

_____
_____
_____
_____

How can you be a better friend to him/her?

_____
_____
_____

Friend Name _____

What qualities make him/her a friend?

_____
_____
_____
_____

How can you be a better friend to him/her?

_____
_____
_____

# Month 5 | Day 4

**Fast:** I did not fast during this month

**Devotion:** 1 Samuel 19 (Read the entire 19th chapter of 1 Samuel)

---

**The Spirit of Jealousy**

Jealousy is cruel, divisive, and evil behavior. Jealousy is the opposite of love and kindness. The Word of God declares, "But if you have bitter jealousy and selfish ambition in your hearts, do not boast and be false to the truth. This is not the wisdom that comes from above but is earthly, unspiritual, demonic (James 3:14-15 ESV).

In 1 Samuel 19, Saul was constantly jealous of David and his success. Unfortunately, some people are jealous of others for no reason other than they hate to see someone else win. Saul's jealousy of David was due to his God-given ability to succeed! David was chosen by God and favored by Him.

**Prayer:** Heavenly Father, I thank You for every victory in my life. Thank You for each success You have given my family and friends. I know that You are in complete control over my life and the lives of others, and there is no need for jealousy to enter my heart. Father, if I am jealous in any way, I ask that You remove it now and forgive me. Also, enable me to see the greatness You have placed in me. In Jesus' name. Amen.

**Activity:** Read 1 Samuel 19

In 1 Samuel 19, Saul sets out to kill David. On the next page, list how

Saul attempts to kill David and each corresponding verse.

_____
_____
_____
_____
_____
_____
_____
_____

Also, list below what happens to the messengers and Saul once they set out to kill David. Read 1 Samuel 19, verses 11-24.

_____
_____
_____
_____
_____
_____

It is important to note that Saul was unsuccessful despite Saul's mission to kill David! Instead of Saul killing David, Saul and his messengers were overtaken by Prophecy, Prayer, and Praise! Do not worry about who is trying to kill you! Continue to prophesy over your life, pray without ceasing, and praise God continually! Hopefully, your enemies will be overtaken with God's spirit and not the evil spirit that is trying to destroy you.

# Month 5 | Day 5

**Fast:** I did not fast during this month.

**Devotion:** 1 Samuel 20:16-17 (ESV) "And Jonathan made a covenant with the house of David, saying, "May the Lord take vengeance on David's enemies. And Jonathan made David swear again by his love for him, for he loved him as he loved his own soul."

---

**Covenant**

David and Jonathan made a Covenant. Covenant is an alliance of friendship; it is an agreement between two people, including God. When a person is born into a natural family, they share the DNA of their mother and father. However, when a covenant is made between two people, the relationship is more robust and more profound than the relationship between blood relatives. For instance, marriage between a man and a woman is a covenant relationship. Genesis 2:24 (ASV) says, "Therefore shall a man leave his father and his mother and shall cleave unto his wife: and they shall be one flesh." A covenant relationship supersedes biological relationships. Jonathan shows us this when he protects David from his father. Jonathan did not allow his father, Saul, to kill David. Apostle Alphonso Montgomery (Pastor and Founder of Led by the Spirit of God Church, Little Rock, AR) once stated, "Blood is thicker than water, but the Spirit is thicker than blood." Thank God for Your spiritual relationships!

**Prayer:** Lord, You made me relational. As I perfect my relationship with You, I ask that You help me grow in my relationship(s) with others. As You bless me with covenant relationships, please give me the strength to be the covenant friend, brother, or sister needed. Thank You, Lord, for residing in my covenant relationship(s). In Jesus' name. Amen.

**Activity:** What does covenant mean to you?

_____
_____
_____

Who are your covenant relationships with? Why?

_____
_____
_____
_____
_____
_____

Remember, life is a journey! Seek God for a covenant relationship that will challenge your walk with God, celebrate your successes with you, defend you in your absence, and always love you no matter what! We need covenant relationships while on our journey!

# Month 5 | Day 6

**Fast:** I did not fast during this month.

**Devotion:** 1 Samuel 21:10-11 (ESV) "And David rose and fled that day from Saul and went to Achish, the king of Gath. And the servants of Achish said to him, "Is not this David, the king of the land? Did they not sing to one another of him in dances, 'Saul has struck down his thousands, and David his ten thousand?'"

**Recognized**

In life, we are faced with defeats and victories! We must be intentional about moving on from our losses while thanking God for the achievements He has given us! Throughout the life of David, he never "tooted his own horn!" Neither should we. Others sang and shouted, "David killed his ten thousand!" They noticed his victorious life. People will also see your wins without you ever saying a word! It is important to note that God chose David, and he was equipped with the courage to do what others were afraid to do.

**Prayer:** Heavenly Father, I thank You for every defeat in my life. I also thank You for every victory in my life! My successes outweigh my losses. I know that You have given me success in every area of my journey. I will forever acknowledge this and give You all the glory! In Jesus' name. Amen.

**Activity:** When was your last time encouraging a family member or friend? Often, we look to be inspired and cheered on; however, we should also be intentional about noticing the victories of others and then singing their praises. Don't just tolerate others but learn to celebrate them also!

Who among your family or friends have overcome battles? What did you witness them overcome? How can you be a better encourager towards them. Use the space below to answer these questions.

1. Friend or family member _____
_____
_____

2. Friend or family member _____
_____
_____

3. Friend or family member _____
_____
_____

4. Friend or family member _____
_____
_____

5. Friend or family member _____
_____
_____

# Month 5 | Day 7

**Fast:** I did not fast during this month.

**Devotion:** 1 Samuel 22 (Read the entire 22nd chapter of 1 Samuel)

**Pay it Forward**

Life is a journey of highs and lows, a journey of hills and valleys, a journey of love and hate. Despite all that you have faced, felt, and feared, you are still here. The enemy, Satan, was unsuccessful in taking your life, liberty, and love. You have remained, not only by telling your story, but also by providing help and protection for someone else.

In 1 Samuel 22, David is on the run from Saul once again. Saul is angry that his son, Jonathan, is a protector of David. Saul, again, is on the rampage to seek out David and murder him. However, David is warned and told to flee and hide. David flees. Furthermore, Doeg informs him of David's coming to Nob, of his being in the company of Ahimelech. Saul then kills Ahimelech and all the priests (eighty-five total) and destroys the city of Nob. Only Abiathar, the son of Ahimelech, escapes. Abiathar then joins David. David assures Abiathar that he will protect him. Despite David literally running for his life and miraculously avoiding being killed by Saul, he ultimately saves someone else. David received loyalty and protection from Saul's son, Jonathan, and paid the same protection forward to Abiathar.

Your life may not be perfect, but you have made it through some of life's most difficult challenges. I have learned to take time to heal and find restoration after challenging trials. There have also been times when facing my most difficult adversities, that I have been motivated to minister to others. I did this as my covenant family and friends have supported me. As you are currently facing a dilemma, keep in mind that someone you know may be facing a more challenging time than you. Pray for them and encourage them. Protect them and pay it forward!

**Prayer:** Lord, I know that all things are working together for my good, and You never make a mistake! Lord, I am thankful for every trial I have faced or may be facing right now. Thank You for the strength to support those who come to me with their problems. Father, give me the wisdom to help those who need me. In Jesus' name. Amen.

**Activity:** As you read and reflect on 1 Samuel 22, pray for people in your life who may be facing difficulties. Pray for their faith to trust in the Lord and for their strength to be renewed. Not only pray for them but contact them. Check on them. Encourage them. The following scriptures should help you keep your mind on this task.

### Proverbs 17:17 (MSG)

Friends love through all kinds of weather, and families stick together in all kinds of trouble.

### Proverbs 18:24 (MSG)

Friends come, and friends go, but a real friend sticks by you like family.

### Proverbs 27:10 (MSG)

Don't leave your friends or parents' friends and run home to your family when things get rough; Better a nearby friend than a distant family.

### Proverbs 27:17 (MSG)

You use steel to sharpen steel, and one friend sharpens another.

### Ecclesiastes 4:9-10 (MSG)

It is better to have a partner than go it alone. Share the work, share the wealth.

And if one falls, the other helps, but if there's no one to help, tough!

# Month 5 | Day 8

**Fast:** I did not fast during this month.

**Devotion:** 1 Samuel 23:9-13 (MSG), "⁹But David got wind of Saul's strategy to destroy him and said to Abiathar, the priest, "Get the Ephod. ¹⁰Then David prayed to God: "God of Israel, I've just heard that Saul plans to come to Keilah and destroy the city because of me. ¹¹Will the city fathers of Keilah turn me over to him? Will Saul come down and do what I've heard? O God, God of Israel, tell me!" God replied, "He's coming down. ¹²And will the head men of Keilah turn me and my men over to Saul?" And God said, "They'll turn you over. ¹³So David and his men got out of there. There were about six hundred of them. They left Keilah and kept moving, going here, there, wherever—always on the move. When Saul was told that David had escaped from Keilah, he called off the raid."

---

**The Choice Is Yours**

How many times have you faced tough decisions? Before making the decision, did you seek the Lord in prayer? Did you seek God through scripture? Were you able to seek wise counsel from a friend or family member? Often, we are faced with situations, unsure of what to do. However, we can ask God for direction just as David did in 1 Samuel 23, verses 9-13.

In 1 Samuel 23, David hears that Saul still has plans to kill him. Because of this, David goes to God in prayer. David says, in verse 11, "Will the city fathers of Keilah turn me over to him? Will Saul come down and do what I've heard? O God, God of Israel, tell me! God replied, "He's coming down." God answers David's questions. Then in verse 12, David also asks, "And will the head men of Keilah turn me and my men over to Saul? And God said, "They'll turn you over." And verse 13 tells us, "So David and his men got out of there."

David asked desperate questions that he needed answers to, and God answered them. However, the key here is although God answers David's questions concerning Saul's pursuit of him and the men turning him over, David was still given the freedom of choice. David could have chosen to stay there and be turned over to Saul. He could have chosen to flee the scene. David decided to move on, the scripture says.

There are times when we have questions for God to answer. For David, God responded immediately. However, ultimately God gave David the freedom of making his own choice to stay or leave. David left. Therefore, David saved his own life.

God has many characteristics. One of them is that He allows us the freedom to make our own choices.

**Prayer:** Father, You are the one and only true living God. You have all power in Your hands. I thank You for answering my prayers. In Jesus' name. Amen.

**Activity:** List the prayer requests that you currently have before the Lord. Were they answered? How did you respond if your prayer request(s) had been answered? What choice did you make?

## THE BUSINESS OF THE MIND

My prayer request(s) is:

_____
_____
_____
_____
_____
_____
_____
_____

Were these requests answered?

_____
_____
_____

What choice did you make after your request(s) were answered?

_____
_____
_____
_____
_____
_____

# Month 5 | Day 9

**Fast:** I did not fast during this month.

**Devotion:** 1 Samuel 24:1-7 (MSG) "When Saul came back after dealing with the Philistines, he was told, "David is now in the wilderness of En Gedi. Saul took three companies—the best he could find in all Israel—and set out searching for David and his men in the region of Wild Goat Rocks. He came to some sheep pens along the road. There was a cave there, and Saul went in to relieve himself. David and his men were huddled far back in the same cave. David's men whispered to him, "Can you believe it? This is the day God was talking about when he said, 'I'll put your enemy in your hands. You can do whatever you want with him.' Quiet as a cat, David crept up and cut off a piece of Saul's royal robe. Immediately, he felt guilty. He said to his men, 'God forbid that I should have done this to my master, God's anointed, that I should so much as raise a finger against him. He's God's anointed!' David held his men in check with these words and wouldn't let them pounce on Saul. Saul got up, left the cave, and went on down the road."

---

**I Could, But I Won't**

Have you ever faced being lied to, talked about negatively, or accused of something of which you were not meeting? Are you facing an enemy who does not want to see you successful? If so, has revenge on your accusers/enemies ever crossed your mind? Being human is more than likely. If you have faced any of these situations, you are not alone. David continued to face the jealousy of Saul while escaping being killed by Saul repeatedly. Nevertheless, when the opportunity came, and Saul's life was in the hands of David, and David could have murdered Saul, he did not.

In today's reading, David was encouraged by his men to take the opportunity to kill Saul. All the men knew how Saul had sought to end David's life. However, David could not do to Saul what Saul had tried, on numerous occasions, to do to him. David recognized Saul as being God's anointed. There are times when God's chosen and called servants do wrong. Their wrongdoing is not pleasing in God's eyes; however, just like David, we should not take matters into our own hands. Allow God to touch your heart, not to seek revenge. Also, allow God to take care of your enemies.

**Prayer:** Heavenly Father, although my enemies may seek to destroy my name, reputation, and life, with Your help, I will not seek revenge. Lord, I ask for Your strength to forgive those who consistently hurt me. I cannot do it without You, Lord. Thank You for a heart of flesh and not of stone to love unconditionally. In Jesus' name. Amen.

**Activity:** As you read 1 Samuel 24, read and meditate on each of the scriptures below and on the next page.

### Matthew 5:38-42 (ESV)

[38] You have heard that it was said, 'An eye for an eye and a tooth for a tooth. [39] But I say to you, do not resist the evil one. But if anyone slaps you on the right cheek, turn to him the other also. [40] And if

anyone would sue you and take your tunic, let him have your cloak as well. ⁴¹ And if anyone forces you to go one mile, go with him two miles. ⁴² Give to the one who begs from you and does not refuse the one who would borrow from you.

### Matthew 5:43-48 (ESV)

⁴³ You have heard that it was said, 'You shall love your neighbor and hate your enemy.' ⁴⁴ But I say to you, love your enemies and pray for those who persecute you, ⁴⁵ so that you may be sons of your Father who is in heaven. For he makes his sun rise on the evil and the good and sends rain on the just and the unjust. ⁴⁶ For if you love those who love you, what reward do you have? Do not even the tax collectors do the same? ⁴⁷ And if you greet only your brothers, what more are you doing than others? Do not even the Gentiles do the same? ⁴⁸ You, therefore, must be perfect, as your heavenly Father is perfect

# Month 5 | Day 10

**Fast:** I did not fast during this month.

**Devotion:** 1 Samuel 25:39 (ESV), "When David heard that Nabal was dead, he said, 'Blessed be the Lord who has avenged the insult I received at the hand of Nabal and has kept back his servant from wrongdoing. The Lord has returned the evil of Nabal on his head.' Then David sent and spoke to Abigail, to take her as his wife."

**Blessed Be the Lord**

We experience both good and bad things in life along our journey. Some of the good we may have deserved. Some of the bad we may have brought upon ourselves. Overall, God is in control of everything. It is challenging, sometimes, to stand by and let God manage it; it is what He wants. The Lord can fight our battles for us. We need only to be still. You may have been wronged, but you do not need to retaliate with revenge. There may be a need to establish boundaries with the individual(s), but the Christ-like thing to do is forgive.

David said, "Blessed be the name of the Lord who has avenged the insult I received at the hand of Nabal and has kept back his servant from wrongdoing." Just as Nabal's wrongdoing caused his fate, those who purposefully plot evil and wickedness on you will have the same. It's all in God's timing. Trust Him to protect you.

**Prayer:** Father, I want to please You. I ask that You lead me, protect me, and give me the wisdom to handle difficult situations that I encounter. Thank You for reminding me that I am blessed and have no need to harm anyone. In Jesus' name. Amen.

**Activity:** As you read through 1 Samuel 25, read and meditate on the following scriptures.

### Exodus 23:5 (ESV)

If you see the donkey of one who hates you lying down under its burden, you shall refrain from leaving him with it; you shall rescue it with him.

### Proverbs 24:29 (ESV)

Do not say, "I will do to him as he has done to me; I will pay the man back for what he has done."

### Proverbs 25:21 (ESV)

If your enemy is hungry, give him bread to eat, and if he is thirsty, give him water to drink.

### Matthew 5:44 (ESV)

But I say to you, love your enemies and pray for those who persecute you.

### Matthew 18:21-22 (ESV)

Then Peter came up and said to him, "Lord, how often will my brother sin against me, and I forgive him? As many as seven times?" Jesus said to him, "I do not say to you seven times, but seventy times seven

# Month 5 | Day 11

**Fast:** I did not fast during this month.

**Devotion:** 1 Samuel 26:21-25 (ESV) "Then Saul said, 'I have sinned. Return, my son David, for I will no more do you harm because my life was precious in your eyes this day. Behold, I have acted foolishly and have made a great mistake.' And David answered and said, 'Here is the spear, O king! Let one of the young men come over and take it.

The Lord rewards every man for his righteousness and his faithfulness, for the Lord gave you into my hand today, and I would not put out my hand against the Lord's anointed. Behold, as your life was precious this day in my sight, so may my life be precious in the sight of the Lord, and may he deliver me out of all tribulation. Then Saul said to David, 'Blessed be you, my son David! You will do many things and will succeed in them.' So, David went his way, and Saul returned to his place."

## Again?

Here Saul and David are *again*! Saul's life is in the hands of David once more, and he has another opportunity to take Saul's life. Not only can he kill Saul, but he can do it with Saul's spear! How revengeful would that be? However, David chooses to spare Saul. Isn't it amazing how David has such a forgiving heart? Saul has repeatedly pursued David with intentions not just to harm him but to end his life! When granted the opportunity for revenge against their number one enemy, most ordinary people would take advantage of it. But not David! 1 Samuel 26:23 (ESV) tells us, "The Lord rewards every man for his righteousness and his faithfulness, for the Lord gave you into my hand today, and I would not put out my hand against the Lord's anointed." We should remember that the Lord rewards all of us for our righteousness and faithfulness, and with God's help, we can live in both! David refused to return to Saul what Saul had tried to do to him…. again! Recognizing that Saul was in authority, David respected Saul's position even though Saul did not respect David's and was entirely jealous of him.

**Prayer:** Father, I desire to please You. I ask for Your help and strength to differ in my heart and behavior towards my enemy. I want to love and forgive like You. When the opportunity arises to harm my enemy like they have harmed me, guide me, and I will follow Your lead. In Jesus' name. Amen.

**Activity:** Fill in the blanks below
(Ezekiel 36:26)
Take out the _____ heart and fill it with a heart of _____.

(Matthew 5:8)
_____ are the _____ in heart for they shall see God.

# Month 5 | Day 12

**Fast:** I did not fast during this month.

**Devotion:** 1 Samuel 27:1 (ESV) "Then David said in his heart, "Now I shall perish one day by the hand of Saul. There is nothing better for me than that I should escape to the land of the Philistines. Then Saul will despair of seeking me any longer within the borders of Israel, and I shall escape out of his hand."

---

**Remember!**

Has God been good to you? Has He forgiven you? Has He saved you from sin? Has He provided for you? If the answer to these four questions is "Yes," then apparently, you know the faithfulness of our Heavenly Father, and there is no reason to doubt Him! David seems to panic and run from Saul again in the today's scripture. If he had only paused to think about the calling and promise of God upon his life to be King, maybe he would not have exerted so much energy running from Saul. Remember, 1 Samuel 16:1 (ESV) says, "The Lord said to Samuel, "How long will you grieve over Saul since I have rejected him from being king over Israel? Fill your horn with oil and go. I will send you to Jesse the Bethlehemite, for I have provided for myself a king among his sons." Also, in 1 Samuel 16:11-13 (ESV), the scripture further states, "Then Samuel said to Jesse, "Are all your sons here?" And he said, " There remains yet the youngest, but behold, he is keeping the sheep." And Samuel said to Jesse, "Send and get him, for we will not sit down till he comes here. And he sent and brought him in. Now he was ruddy and had beautiful eyes and was handsome.

And the Lord said, "Arise, anoint him, for this is he. Then Samuel took the horn of oil and anointed him amid his brothers. And the Spirit of the Lord rushed upon David from that day forward. And Samuel arose and went to Ramah.

We often only focus on the test or trial currently before us. In the future, do your best while not ignoring the present circumstance; remember the call, grace, and favor upon your life. Just as David was chosen to be King over God's chosen people, you are selected for a particular destiny.

**Prayer:** Lord, I am thankful that You called and chose me; I praise You for picking me out to serve You. Father, forgive me for neglecting to remind myself of Your faithfulness. Help me to remember Your love as I face everyday life. Help me to remember the call You have placed on my life. Also, Father, with Your help, I will never forget what You have done for me. In Jesus' name. Amen.

**Activity:** On the next page, write the situation or trial you are currently facing; also, write a scripture, or scriptures, of your choice that reminds you that God is with you. Then meditate on each of them.

## THE BUSINESS OF THE MIND

| My Current Situation or Trial | Scriptures that Minister to Me |
|---|---|
| | |
| | |
| | |
| | |
| | |
| | |
| | |

# Month 5 | Day 13

**Fast:** I did not fast during this month.

**Devotion:** 1 Samuel 28:17-19 (ESV) "[17]The Lord has done to you as he spoke by me, for the Lord has torn the kingdom out of your hand and given it to your neighbor, David. [18]Because you did not obey the voice of the Lord and did not carry out his fierce wrath against Amalek, therefore the Lord has done this thing to you this day. [19]Moreover, the Lord will give Israel also with you into the hand of the Philistines, and tomorrow you and your sons shall be with me. The Lord will give the army of Israel also into the hand of the Philistines."

---

**To Obey or Not to Obey**

Sir Frances Bacon once said, "Knowledge is power." That statement is true. However, how many blessings have we forfeited due to relying on knowledge? Sometimes we rely on our own knowledge, leading to disobedience to God. When we obey our Heavenly Father, by hearing His voice or reading His Holy Word, we gain more power for ourselves and those closest to us. Saul's disobedience to God's commands hurts him, his family, and Israel. We need to realize that our obedience and/or disobedience affects others. Which will you choose to do?

**Prayer:** Lord, I thank You for the opportunity to live for You and to serve You. I ask that You forgive me for any disobedience to Your word that I have displayed. Lord, strengthen me to do Your will along my journey of life. I will forever give You the glory, honor, and praise. In Jesus' name. Amen.

THE LIFE AND JOURNEY

**Activity:** Read the entire chapter of 1 Samuel 28. Answer the questions below.

1. When Saul inquired of the Lord, did the Lord answer Saul? (vs. 6) Yes or No (circle one).

2. Since the Lord did not answer Saul, who did Saul turn to? (vs. 7)
_____
_____

3. Who did Saul ask the medium to "bring up" for him? (vs. 11)
    a. Jesus
    b. Samuel
    c. Elijah

4. List the three (3) things Samuel says will happen due to the disobedience of Saul? (vs. 19)
    1._____
    2._____
    3._____

Why is obedience to God important to you?
_____
_____
_____
_____

# Month 5 | Day 14

**Fast:** I did not fast during this month.

**Devotion:** 1 Samuel 29:6-7 (ESV) "Then Achish called David and said to him, 'As the Lord lives, you have been honest, and to me, it seems right that you should march out and in with me in the campaign, for I have found nothing wrong in you from the day of your coming to me to this day. Nevertheless, the lords disapprove of you. So go back now, and go peaceably, that you may please the lords of the Philistines."

---

**Rejected...Again**

Rejection is the opposite of acceptance. Throughout life, we are rejected for several reasons. Some reasons for being denied are race, religion, social status, and education – or the lack thereof. However, others have been dismissed for no apparent reason. In 1 Samuel, Saul is rejected by God because of his disobedience. Saul rejects David because of jealousy. In today's reading, David is rejected by the Philistines because they assume David will join in with their enemies to defeat them. Achish tries to explain to the lords of the Philistines that David has not done anything wrong and can be trusted. Nevertheless, the Philistines are adamant and refuse to accept David going to war with them. David then travels back to Achish's land, which Achish initially allowed David and his men to live.

**Prayer:** Heavenly Father, thank You for accepting me the way I am; I am not perfect. I make mistakes. I fail You at times. Father, help me to continue growing in You each day. As I love my neighbor as myself, I thank You for the strength to work through any rejection that I may face. In Jesus' name. Amen.

**Activity:** Below write reasons that have caused you to be rejected by others:

_____
_____
_____
_____


Have you ever rejected anyone? If so, why? Write your reason(s) below.

_____
_____
_____
_____
_____
_____


Regardless of being rejected, declare, I am accepted by God! Meditate on the next page's scriptures today:

### Romans 15:7 ESV

Therefore, welcome one another as Christ has welcomed you, for the glory of God.

### Luke 10:16 ESV

The one who hears you hears me, and the one who rejects you rejects me, and the one who rejects me rejects him who sent me.

### John 3:16 ESV

For God so loved the world, that he gave his only Son, that whoever believes in him should not perish but have eternal life.

### John 17:26 ESV

I made known to them your name, and I will continue to make it known that the love with which you have loved me may be in them, and I in them.

# Month 5 | Day 15

**Fast:** I did not fast during this month.

**Devotion:** 1 Samuel 30:1-6 (ESV) "Now when David and his men came to Ziklag on the third day, the Amalekites had made a raid against the Negeb and Ziklag. They had overcome Ziklag and burned it with fire and taken captive the women and all who were in it, both small and great. They killed no one but carried them off and went their way. And when David and his men came to the city, they found it burned with fire, and their wives and sons and daughters were taken captive. Then David and the people with him raised their voices and wept until they had no more strength to weep. David's two wives were also taken captive, Ahinoam of Jezreel and Abigail, the widow of Nabal of Carmel. And David was greatly distressed, for the people spoke of stoning him because everyone was bitter in soul, each for his sons and daughters. But David strengthened himself in the Lord his God."

---

### It's OK...Encourage Yourself

Again, life is a journey. David encountered various situations throughout his life. Some of the good that happened, David deserved. Some of the bad he earned also. However, no matter what David faced, he was always resilient. He always found a way to bounce back and win his battle. David's life is a testimony for those who have faced difficulties on our journey called life. We can learn from him. We can find strength in the Lord our God.

# THE LIFE AND JOURNEY

**Prayer:** Lord, I thank You for my very life. Thank You for my battles, struggles, fears, and losses. Without them, I would not know Your strength. Lord, thank You for Your strength as I journey throughout life. I know it is You and only You who can and will give me the victory no matter what I face. I will give You the honor and praise for every win. In Jesus' name, I pray. Amen.

**Activity:** Upon the return home of David and his men, they find their wives and children taken by the enemy and everything destroyed by fire. In 1 Samuel 30:6 (ESV), the Bible says, "And David was greatly distressed, for the people spoke of stoning him because all the people were bitter in soul, each for his sons and daughters. But David strengthened himself in the Lord his God. At first, David is distressed. Then, after David strengthens himself in the Lord, he conquerors his enemies and gets all that belongs to him back. In the following areas, write how you have felt when facing a difficult situation. Also, note how you have felt after praying and seeking God for His strength.

1. Trial Facing:

_____

How I felt during my trial before seeking God's strength:

_____
_____
_____

## THE BUSINESS OF THE MIND

How I felt during my trial after seeking God's strength:

_____
_____
_____

2. Trial Facing:

_____

How I felt during my trial before seeking God's strength:

_____
_____
_____

How I felt during my trial after seeking God's strength:

_____
_____
_____

Additional notes:

_____
_____
_____
_____
_____

# Month 5 | Day 16

**Fast:** I did not fast during this month.

**Devotion:** I Samuel 31:4-6 (ESV) "⁴Then Saul said to his armor-bearer, "Draw your sword, and thrust me through with it, lest these uncircumcised come and thrust me through, and mistreat me. But his armor-bearer would not, for he feared greatly. Therefore, Saul took his sword and fell upon it. ⁵And when his armor-bearer saw that Saul was dead, he also fell upon his sword and died with him. ⁶Thus Saul died, and his three sons, and his armor-bearer, and all his men, on the same day together."

---

**The Price of Disobedience**

How did Saul get here in 1 Samuel 31? Why did Saul, his sons, his men, and armor-bearer die? These are all questions that can be answered by going back to chapter 28. In 1 Samuel 28:18-19 (ESV) it says the following:

> Because you did not obey the voice of the Lord and did not carry out his fierce wrath against Amalek, therefore the Lord has done this thing to you this day. Moreover, the Lord will give Israel also with you into the hand of the Philistines, and tomorrow you and your sons shall be with me. The Lord will give the army of Israel also into the hand of the Philistines.

Because Saul did not obey the voice of the Lord, the following occurrences transpired:

1. He was rejected as King of Israel (1 Samuel 15:23)
2. His men were killed (1 Samuel 31:1)
3. His sons were killed (1 Samuel 31:2)
4. He committed self-murder or suicide (1 Samuel 31:4)
5. His armor-bearer committed self-murder or suicide (1 Samuel 31:5)

These things were a direct result of Saul's disobedience to the Lord. It is essential, as a Believer, to obey God's word. Otherwise, disobedience will affect the individual and those connected to the individual. Just think: Had Saul obeyed the voice of the Lord, he would not have been rejected as king. Had Saul obeyed the voice of the Lord, his men may have lived longer, his sons' lives may have been spared, the armor-bearer of Saul may have lived on. Had Saul obeyed the voice of the Lord, Saul, himself, may have continued to live; and upon his death, he would have been buried in a dignified manner rather than being burned and his bones buried. Remember that obedience is better than sacrifice as you travel on life's journey.

**Prayer:** Lord, I thank You and praise You for the lives of my family members, my friends, and my very own. I ask that You forgive me of any area(s) of disobedience in my life. I want to pass on blessings to my loved ones and not curses. Father, give me the strength to obey Your word. I will continue to live for You, praise You and glorify You with my life. In the name of Jesus, I pray. Amen.

# THE BUSINESS OF THE MIND

**Activity:** Fill in the area (or areas), on the below and on the next page, where you have been disobedient to God (His Word). Also, note the area (or areas) where you have obeyed His Word.

Area(s) of Disobedience

| |
|---|
| 1. |
| 2. |
| 3. |
| 4. |
| 5. |

How did disobedience to God make you feel?

___

___

___

___

What life lessons did disobedience teach you?

___

___

___

___

Area(s) of Obedience

| |
|---|
| 1. |
| 2. |
| 3. |
| 4. |
| 5. |

How did obedience to God make you feel?

_____
_____
_____
_____
_____

What life lessons did obedience teach you?

_____
_____
_____
_____
_____

# MONTH 6

## "23"
### The Business of the Mind

Last month's reading will provide perspective for this month's devotions. Several lessons can be learned from those chapters in 1 Samuel. Now, we will use those chapters as a foundation for what we will cover this month. Psalm 23 is not only one of the most popular Psalms, but it is one of the most recited scriptures in the Bible. Often, we hear this Psalm at funerals, but this Psalm is so much more than a sad psalm. This Psalm of David reflects the *life and journey* of David as he exclaims how good God has been to him. It is a blueprint that we can use each day of our lives; it can help set the tone for each day.

This month, set aside six days to go through the six verses in this Psalm – one verse for each day. As you fast each day, pray that God reveals to you how these principles can be applied on each day of this journey and each day after.

## "23"

[1] The LORD is my shepherd; I shall not want.
[2] He makes me lie down in green pastures. He leads me beside still waters.
[3] He restores my soul. He leads me in paths of righteousness for his name's sake.
[4] Even though I walk through the valley of the shadow of death, I will fear no evil, for you are with me; your rod and your staff, They comfort me.
[5] You prepare a table before me in the presence of my enemies; you anoint my head with oil; My cup overflows.
[6] Surely goodness and mercy shall follow me all the days of my life, and I shall dwell in the house of the LORD Forever.

# Month 6 | Day 1

**Fast:** No meat; no bread

**Devotion:** Psalm 23:1 "The LORD is my shepherd; I shall not want."

---

David starts this Psalm off in great fashion by doing several things. Understanding that David, himself, was a shepherd tending to his father's sheep, David establishes creditability as he sets the stage with the first of nine analogies by writing that "the Lord is my shepherd." I imagine David speaking of *humility* and *accountability* in part A of this text. This reference can imply that even a shepherd needs a shepherd. Another way of saying this is that even a leader needs a leader. I am a husband and a father: the leader in my home, the head of my household. David tells me that the single, most important thing I can do to lead my family is to be accountable. If I am to lead, I should first learn to follow. In *The Master Plan of Evangelism*, Dr. Robert Coleman states, "no one can ever be a leader until he has learned to follow a leader." David looks to the Lord as his shepherd and his leader in the spiritual sense. We should take that same approach and look to the Father, through the holy spirit, as our leader. Furthermore, we could also surround ourselves with like-minded individuals (in my case - men who are also husbands and fathers) seeking direction from God.

Dr. Tony Evans explains the concept of Heaven's Embassy in *Kingdom Man* in that the church should be a haven from the world serving as a representation of heaven on earth. Submitting to a local church and its leadership is a way to seek and accept accountability and

## "23"

surround yourself with like-minded individuals. And while seeking and accepting responsibility, it will require exercising humility.

Continuing to look at the relationship between shepherd and sheep, we understand that shepherds provide for their sheep. So, a shepherd is a provider. A shepherd provides protection, direction, nutrition, and the list can go on. However, looking back at the text, we can take it that David is saying, "The Lord is my provider, so I shall not want." Take time to reflect on 1 Samuel and write down instances where God provided for David. In your reflections, consider this question: if the same God who provided for David is the same God I serve, how might God make provisions for me? Additionally, reflect on who you are currently accountable to and individuals you could be responsible to based on their walk with God.

<u>1 Samuel 17:46-51</u>
<u>God provided David with victory over Goliath.</u>

## THE BUSINESS OF THE MIND

# Month 6 | Day 2

Fast: No meat; no bread

Devotion: Psalm 23:2 "He makes me lie down in green pastures. He leads me beside still waters."

---

First, as we consider this passage, examine the word *He*. The *He* was established in verse 1 as *My Shepherd – My Provider*. Continuing in verse 2, He, *My Shepherd – My Provider*, makes me lie down in green pastures. This implies that *My Shepherd – My Provider* provides my needs: food as represented in green pastures, drinking water described as still waters, and rest implied in maketh me lie down.

There are two adjectives to note in this text: *green* and *still*. Green describes the type of pastures and *still* is describing the type of waters. Understanding that pastures are "lands covered with grass and other low plants suitable for grazing," the adjective of green is conveying a plentiful harvest for the sheep. The text did not say dry pastures or scarce pastures. It specifically explains that the pastures were abundant and suitable. Furthermore, sheep will not usually lie down until they are satisfied. I imagine David is delighted with how his provider has met his needs; he has met his needs in abundance.

As a shepherd leads his sheep through the wilderness, we know that water appears in several types of ways in nature. These include waterfalls, raging waters, fast-flowing rivers, and so on. However, the text says that "he leads me beside *still* waters." One reason the shepherd would lead the sheep beside the water in the first place is for the sheep to drink. If the seas were not calm and still, but rather wild and raging, the sheep would not only have been unable to drink, but the sheep could have been captured by the raging waters and drowned. Therefore, we can consider *still waters*, as well as *green pastures*, not only speaking of abundance, but also as meaning an environment of peace and safety.

I can imagine that the shepherd strategically searches for this particular type of environment. The Bible says in Psalm 46:10 to "Be still and know that I am God." This can mean that we should stop being so busy being busy so that we can hear God's voice. If we do not stop with our busyness – always being in such a rush – we could get his voice confused with the ambient noises of this world. We will hear God when we prepare our environment to hear God's voice. Examples could be waking up earlier than usual, before our family wakes up, to position ourselves to hear his voice. This could be also present itself as stepping away from the rush at work for a few moments or staying up a little later than usual after our family has gone to sleep.

Finally, looking at the idea of God (our shepherd) leading us, I visualize our master going before us in the wilderness with an ax or a machete creating a path or a walkway. I can see him, then, come back to get us, his sheep, and lead us on the way he just created. As this analogy is translated, God (our shepherd) goes before us, preparing the people, situations, and environments we will face throughout the day before we even start on our day. He then returns and walks with us to lead us throughout our day.

Consider the final analogy presented in today's devotion regarding the idea of God, our shepherd, leading us. Imagine this day as the wilderness, and imagine God, our shepherd, preparing the people, situations, and environments you will encounter today. Before we even leave the house, he has prepared the way. He then comes back to walk through the day with us. Visualize this scenario today and remember that God is walking before you today.

# Month 6 | Day 3

**Fast:** No meat; no bread

**Devotion:** Psalm 23:3 "He restores my soul. He leads me in paths of righteousness for his name's sake."

---

Restore means to bring back or reinstate. The soul is considered our mind, will, and emotions. I can't help but think about when David slept with Bathsheba in 2 Samuel and afterward had her husband killed. To me, David is saying here that God (*My* shepherd) will restore me. Though I've sinned and fallen short of his glory, I believe *He* will bring back or reinstate my mind, my will, and my emotions. Also, referring back to 1 Samuel 19, he could be thinking of when the Amalekites invaded their town and took their wives and children as captives. David recovered, brought back, and restored his family with God's provision. Just as God restored David and the things that impacted his mind, will, and emotions, there is nothing you have done that is so bad that God can't restore your soul if you are willing.

When we read "For his namesake," I think back to the path that God created in Psalm 23:2. As our shepherd goes before us (his sheep) to prepare the way, he picks up weeds and removes poisonous vegetation in preparation for us to come through safely. The path that our shepherd creates for us will not lead us to destruction, but instead, it will lead us to success and victory. He will lead us in such a way that his name will be glorified. We will have victory, not for ourselves and not because we are so good, but because we proudly and sincerely live for Him. Knowing that we live for God, when people see the path that

## "23"

we walk (and have walked), his name *will* be glorified.

Think about the things that you want God to restore you from. Think about the things that may have your mind overloaded, your will in question, your emotions everywhere. Write those items on the lines below.

God, I would like You to restore my soul; I have been weak in the following areas:

_____

_____

_____

_____

_____

_____

_____

Now, Lord, I am asking that you lead me in paths of righteousness for Your name's sake. In Jesus' name. Amen.

# Month 6 | Day 4

**Fast:** No meat; no bread

**Devotion:** Psalm 23:4 "Even though I walk through the valley of the shadow of death, I will fear no evil, for you are with me; your rod and your staff, they comfort me."

---

The valley of the shadow of death can be interpreted as a *dark place*. We often have *dark moments* and dark places in our life and journey. When these moments occur, we often want to hurry through those moments, or we tend to want them to quickly leave. Notice the text, however, says *walk*. It does not say hurry or run. This notion is important because we should not rush through those dark times; those times are a part of the process. When we rush, we tend to make mistakes. However, we are more observant when we walk. When we walk in darkness, we must also rely on and be more observant of our faith – for we walk by faith and not by sight. And, if *My Shepherd* is leading me through a dark valley, there must be something He wants me to witness or encounter. Let me walk, be observant, and identify what He wants me to see.

Additionally, David says he will fear no evil. He will fear no evil, one, because God did not give him a spirit of fear, which we established in one of our foundational scriptures. I can't help but think he will fear no evil because his shepherd, going back to verse 2, has already prepared the grounds that he will walk on throughout the journey. If we trust God, there is no reason to doubt His provision or the path He created. Finally, David says he will *fear no evil* because he

# "23"

recognizes and acknowledges that *Thou* are with him. The shepherd doesn't just make the path; he then walks and leads the sheep along the way.

When we think of the shepherd/sheep analogy, it is essential not to rush through this particular text. We should carefully consider the purpose of a rod and a staff.

A *rod* is used to fight off lions, bears, and other predators that may try to attack the sheep. We see, then, that the shepherd doesn't just provide provision, but the shepherd also provides protection. Furthermore, as a shepherd leads his sheep, sheep tend to wander off the path. So, a shepherd has a *staff* to reach out and hook a sheep by its neck or other body part and bring it back to the flock. These tools, this process, these symbols of authority are what David referenced at the end of this verse when it said "…*they comfort me.*"

Consider the following questions as you go throughout today. Use the space provided to write the answers to the specific questions.

What are some of the dark valleys that you may be walking through?

_____

_____

_____

_____

What do you think God wants you to see during those dark moments?

_____

_____

## THE BUSINESS OF THE MIND

_____

_____

Are you a constant wanderer?

_____

_____

What do you think the root of your wandering is?

_____

_____

_____

_____

_____

# Month 6 | Day 5

**Fast:** No meat; no bread

**Devotion:** Psalm 23:5 "You prepare a table before me in the presence of my enemies; you anoint my head with oil; my cup overflows."

---

As the sheep graze on green pastures, the shepherd keeps their watch – as we remember the rod from verse four of this text and its purpose, lets recall the conversation between David and King Saul in 1 Samuel 17:34-36 (Month 5 Day 2) where David explained how he protected his father's sheep. This process even goes on while the sheep are eating. This represents *a table prepared in the presence of my enemies*. For us, God can provide us with a platform in front of those who may have rejected us. More than a platform, God will also prepare and deliver provisions and victories in the presence of our enemies, and he will make those who routed against us witness it. This happens not for us to get a cold heart or become boastful, but so that God can be glorified.

Anoint means to smear or rub with something. This process happened to David in 1 Samuel 16 (Month 5 - Day 1) as David was tending to his father's sheep. Samuel came to anoint one of Jesse's sons. All of Jesse's sons lined up, except David, and the oil didn't work on any of those lined up. Samuel was puzzled, thinking there must be someone else. David was later brought in. Samuel knew this was the next king as the oil was anointed onto David. The oil had worked. So, his reference to his head being anointed with oil is, first, literal.

Oil was used as a topical treatment in the agricultural realm to help the healing process of scratches, scrapes, and bruises. As sheep graze in the green pastures, they sometimes wander while grazing. Sometimes, the pastures are unprepared and can cause the sheep to scratch the tops of their heads on weeds, stickers, rocks, and other aspects of nature. Once the shepherd gets his sheep back from wandering, he would apply oil on their heads to help heal those newly formed wounds. Another practical, literal instance of anointing the sheep's head with oil.

Additionally, oil has been used as a natural repellent for flying insects. During periods throughout the year – particularly the summer months, nose flies tend to *bug* sheep to the point of potential danger. The moisture from the sheep's noses attracts these specific flies and other flying insects. The flies tend to fly around the sheep's noses in an attempt to lay eggs in the sheep's noses. This is very problematic for sheep as infection, inflammation, and general irritation will become evident for the sheep if the flies are successful in their attempt to lay eggs. As flies fly around the sheep's nose, land on the sheep's nose, and crawl up the sheep's nose, it is simply irritating to the sheep as they have no hands to fan away the flying insects. As a reaction, the sheep will tend to bang their heads against trees, walls, fences, and other items to try and stop the irritation. Can you imagine how irritating and dangerous this must be? Imagine having a situation or circumstance continuing to stay in your face *bugging* you, attempting to get inside you, attempting to irritate you, attempting to make you cause undue harm to yourself. This is where the anointing of the oil is so powerful. During this time of the year, a good shepherd would apply oil to the sheep's nose so that the oil could serve as the natural repellent limiting and preventing the nose flies from causing harm to the sheep.

As we see this, I can't help but to think of how our shepherd continues to save us from ourselves. We wander; he pulls us in with his staff. When we continue to wander with more significant potential to be harmed by lions and bears, he protects us. When we get *bugged* and beat ourselves up, he anoints us and keeps us harm.

Finally, he anoints us and allows our cups to run over. This cup is representative of the anointing. The source of the blessing is the Holy Spirit, and its flow is everlasting.

What tables have God prepared for you in the presence of your enemies?

_____
_____
_____


What wounds has God healed for you?

_____
_____
_____


In what ways has God kept you from beating yourself up?

_____
_____
_____

# Month 6 | Day 6

**Fast:** (Last Day) – no food; only liquid

**Devotion:** Psalm 23:6 "Surely goodness and mercy shall follow me all the days of my life, and I shall dwell in the house of the LORD forever."

---

As this text starts with "Surely," this tells me there are no doubts. Indeed, God's goodness and mercy are sufficient for me. It has been enough for David through his life and journey as we remember and think of examples from 1 Samuel. David knew, like Isaiah, that no weapon formed against him would prosper (Isaiah 54:17). He understood that the weapons *would* be formed, but they would not prosper. He knew he was fighting with the proper armor.

A familiar analogy in the Bible comes from Ephesians 6, which talks about the *whole armor of God*. We see that our loins are girt about with truth; our breastplate is righteousness. We have our "feet shod with the preparation of the gospel of peace." There's the "shield of faith, wherewith ye shall be able to quench all the fiery darts of the wicked." Finally, we "take the helmet of salvation, and the sword of the Spirit, which is the word of God." While this should give us great confidence, there is one thing to note; our backs are exposed! However, Psalms 23:6 assures us that there are no doubts. *Surely*, God's goodness and his mercy are *following* us. God goes before us, and his grace, integrity, and mercy *follow* us all the days of our life. And we will dwell in the house of the Lord forever. This is a promise, and indeed, I believe it.

As we complete these six verses in Psalm 23, note that verses 1, 2,

## "23"

and 3 have something in common with verse six. In these verses, David is talking about God and is speaking in general terms to an audience, which leaves verses four and five, to which David is talking to God. I can't help but think that as David is talking about God, he couldn't help but think of the favor that God had shown to him throughout his life; so, he turns his attention from the audience and points it directly to God crying out using these analogies as examples of the favor God has shown him. As he comes to an end in verse six, I can see David trying to recompose himself, turning his attention back to the audience.

As you go about your day today, randomly look behind you and smile as you visualize God's *goodness* and *mercy* following you.

# MONTH 7

## Weak but Willing

*The Business of the Mind*

To introduce this month's devotions, let's set the stage for the upcoming studies for the next eight days. In Matthew Chapter 26, Christ Jesus is preparing to fulfill His ultimate sacrifice. Before we begin the study of verses 36-46 of this same chapter, let's build up to our first verse in this study.

First, the plot to kill Jesus is set in verses 1-5 (ESV). In verses 6-13 (ESV), Jesus is anointed with expensive oil from an alabaster box. Then, in verses 14-16 (ESV), Judas plans to betray Jesus. We read of the Passover in verses 17-25 (ESV). The Lord's Supper in verses 26-29 (ESV). And lastly, Jesus Tells of Peter's Denial in verses 30-35 (ESV).

The previously mentioned events lead to Jesus' life being sacrificed for the entire world's sins. Jesus was born to die. It was the design of our Heavenly Father, and it was also the destiny of Christ. It is also important to note that the Lord also ordered our lives.

Often, we make plans. When those plans do not succeed, we say, "Well, on to plan 'B'!" However, with God, there is always plan 'A'. His plan 'A' was for Christ to live, die and live again! Because of God's perfect plan of redemption, we can live an abundant life.

# Month 7 | Day 1

**Fast:** No Meat

**Devotion:** Matthew 26:36 "Then Jesus went with them to a place called Gethsemane, and he said to his disciples, 'Sit here, while I go over there and pray."

## The Place

As Jesus enters His last days of life, can you imagine how He feels? Before giving his life (no man takes Jesus' life), it's essential to understand that He visits the Garden of Gethsemane. The scripture tells us that Jesus visited Gethsemane before He was to be betrayed and crucified. Let's take into consideration the significance of Gethsemane. The meaning of Gethsemane is "oil press." Here, in Gethsemane, Jesus is "pressed" to pray. Jesus left His disciples to do one thing: Pray. When the pressure becomes too heavy, we must do as Jesus did and commune with our Heavenly Father. Gethsemane was Jesus' place of prayer. It is essential that we have a specific area of prayer.

**Prayer:** Father, even though times may be difficult, and the pressures of life may be heavy, I thank You for all that You are to me and for all that You do to sustain me. Lord, I will continue to honor You with a life of prayer. In Jesus' name. Amen.

**Activity:** Discover your place of prayer. Once you have found it, make it a habit of praying there daily. My *place of prayer is* _____

# Month 7 | Day 2

**Fast:** No Meat

**Devotion:** Matthew 26:37 (ESV) "And taking with him Peter and the two sons of Zebedee; he began to be sorrowful and troubled."

---

Is there something that makes you feel sorrowful? Is there anything that troubles you? It is understandable if you answered yes to one or both questions. Jesus began to be sorrowful and troubled, just as you and I often feel. I am grateful that the writer lets us know this; it gives us insight that if our Lord and Savior, Jesus, was troubled in His humanity, you and I will also face difficulties. However, Romans 8:37 (ESV) says, "No, in all these things we are more than conquerors through him who loved us."

**Prayer:** Lord, I must be honest. I am facing trials of every kind; I am sorrowful and troubled. Lord, I need You now. I need Your strength and peace to comfort me at this moment. I thank You, Lord, for hearing my prayer. I know You will never leave me or forsake me. In Jesus' name. Amen.

**Activity:** As believers, we are human; therefore, we experience every emotion at some point in time. On a scale of 1 to 6, write the number (on the next page) beside each emotion. The lowest number is the emotion you experience the least, and the highest number is the emotion you experience the most. This will help you see which feeling you experience most minor and which emotion you experience most.

# WEAK BUT WILLING

Happiness _____ Sadness _____ Fear _____

Disgust _____ Anger _____ Surprise _____

Depending on which emotion you experience the most, Sadness, Fear, Disgust, or Anger, you may need to visit your "Gethsemane" or your place of prayer and ask God for His help in dealing with the emotion(s). Also, be mindful that God has provided trained professionals to help us sort out our emotions as well.

# Month 7 | Day 3

**Fast:** No Meat

**Devotion:** Matthew 26:38 (ESV) "Then he said to them, "My soul is very sorrowful, even to death; remain here, and watch with me."

In this verse, we read what Jesus says. He says, "My soul is very sorrowful, even to death." This is important to note because Jesus is sincere. He does not hide what He is feeling; He does not deny what He is feeling. Jesus is upfront and open about His current emotional state, and He communicates this to His disciples.

**Prayer:** Lord, I need You to bless my soul. In Jesus' name. Amen.

**Activity:** Read and Meditate on the Scriptures on the scriptures below throughout today.

### Psalm 23:3 ESV
He restores my soul. He leads me in paths of righteousness for his name's sake.

### Ezekiel 18:4 ESV
Behold, all souls are mine; the soul of the father as well as the soul of the son is mine: the soul who sins shall die.

### Matthew 16:26 ESV
For what will it profit a man if he gains the whole world and forfeits his soul? Or what shall a man give in return for his soul?

**3 John 1:2 ESV**

Beloved, I pray that all may go well with you and that you may be in good health, as it goes well with your soul.

**Mark 8:36 ESV**

For what does it profit a man to gain the whole world and forfeit his soul?

# Month 7 | Day 4

**Fast:** No Meat

**Devotion:** Matthew 26:39 (ESV) "And going a little farther he fell on his face and prayed, saying, "My Father, if it is possible, let this cup pass from me; nevertheless, not as I will, but as you will."

Jesus, while in Gethsemane, leaves His disciples, while going a little farther away from them, falls on His face and prays; Jesus shares His most profound emotion with His Father. After He shares His desires, He quickly puts what He wants aside and declares that the will of His Father be done. We often face life's challenges and want our desires to be fulfilled. This is a natural response. However, when we are like Jesus, we want the will of our Heavenly Father to be fulfilled.

**Prayer:** Father, I honor who You are. I know You have my best interest at heart. Lord, although what I am facing is difficult, I know You are perfect, and so is Your will for my life. I accept Your will. May Your will be done. In Jesus' name. Amen.

**Activity:** In what area(s) are you playing "tug-of-war" with God? My will. His will. My will. His will. On the next page, write what you desire to happen in your life and then dedicate each of those areas to the Lord and ask Him to lead you in the way you should go.

# WEAK BUT WILLING

My will is to _____
_____
_____
_____
_____
_____

My will is to _____
_____
_____
_____
_____
_____

My will is to _____
_____
_____
_____
_____
_____

However, not my will, but Your will be done in my life.

# Month 7 | Day 5

**Fast:** No Meat

**Devotion:** Matthew 26:40 (ESV) "And he came to the disciples and found them sleeping. And he said to Peter, 'So, could you not watch with me one hour?'"

---

Has the Lord ever displayed His power in your life? Has He empowered you to do something you never thought you could? In the Gospel of Matthew, chapter 14, verses 26-28, we read, the following:

But when the disciples saw him walking on the sea, they were terrified, and said, "It is a ghost!" and they cried out in fear. But immediately, Jesus spoke to them, saying, "Take heart; it is I. Do not be afraid." And Peter answered him, "Lord, if it is you, command me to come to you on the water. He said, "Come." So Peter got out of the boat, walked on water, and came to Jesus.

What a miracle and a once-in-a-lifetime opportunity for Peter to walk on water just as Jesus did! The power of Jesus made it possible for Peter to do the impossible! Jesus enables Peter to walk on water, but Peter cannot stay awake for one hour to watch with Him. Let's not be guilty of receiving the blessings of the Lord while neglecting to serve Him.

**Prayer:** Lord, I know that You are always with me, and I thank You for never leaving me. I pray specifically for my family member(s) and close friend(s) who share my hardships. Father, bless them for their faithfulness to You and also to me. As they share in my sorrows and trials, gift them to have strength. Also, thank You for granting me the power to watch and pray with them in their times of need. In Jesus' name. Amen.

**Activity:** Jesus asked the disciples, "So could you not watch with me one hour?" In this text, the word watch is a verb that requires action. A watch means keeping awake, being spiritually alert. The Bible declares in 1 Corinthians 16:13, "Watch ye, stand fast in the faith, quit you like men, be strong." For this activity, the list below is for you to write the name of family or friends who watch with you as you pray through your adversity. As you list their names, pray for them, and also be sure that you watch as they endure their hardships.

Names of those that watch for and with me as I pray:

_____

_____

_____

_____

_____

_____

# Month 7 | Day 6

**Fast:** No Meat

**Devotion:** Matthew 26:41 (ESV) "Watch and pray that you may not enter into temptation. The spirit indeed is willing, but the flesh is weak."

---

Jesus provides two instructions to His disciples in this verse: 1) Watch. 2) Pray. As we read, these commands are communicated to keep them from temptation. We are often tempted in a variety of ways. Some are tempted in lust; some are tempted with alcohol and drug addiction. Whatever your temptation, it is there to distract you from God and His plan for your life. However, you do not have to give in to that temptation. As God's spirit lives in you, He will strengthen you. Remember, the flesh, or humanity, is weak. The Spirit is willing.

**Prayer:** Heavenly Father, I desire to do Your will; I want to please You. However, there are times I get weak. I have moments when I am not at my best. In those moments, I need Your guidance and the strength of the Holy Spirit. Thank You for providing me with the power to do what is necessary to please You. In Jesus' name. Amen.

**Activity:** The next page has several keywords from this scripture text. Write the Biblical definition to each word. This will help in understanding their importance. Please feel free to use the commentary (or resource) of your choice.

The definition of Watch

# WEAK BUT WILLING

_____

The definition of Pray

_____

The definition of Temptation

_____

The definition of Spirit

_____

The definition of Flesh

_____

# Month 7 | Day 7

**Fast:** No Meat

**Devotion:** Matthew 26:42-44 (ESV) "[42]Again, for the second time, He went away and prayed, "My Father, if this cannot pass unless I drink it, Your will be done." [43]And again he came and found them sleeping, for their eyes were heavy. [44]So, leaving them again, he went away and prayed for the third time, repeating the same words."

---

In life, we often face decisions and difficulties that we pray about. We seek God for His guidance, strength, and wisdom. We pray concerning our dilemma once; then, we go to God twice. If you have done this, it is ok. We can take Jesus' example. He went to His Father again and talked to Him a second time. It is normal to deal with the daily hardships of obeying God's word and pleasing Him in our humanity. In times like that, we may need to follow the lead of Christ and pray *again*! If we are going to deny ourselves, take up our cross and follow Him, we may need to...pray a *third* time. Remember, there is nothing weak about taking another shot at praying *again* concerning the faced situation.

**Prayer:** Father, I thank You for hearing my plea. I come to You *again* concerning my situation. Lord, I need Your strength as I go through my daily walk with You. As I pray concerning my life as a believer, I desire to do Your will. Not my will but Yours be done in every area of my life. In Jesus' name. Amen.

## WEAK BUT WILLING

**Activity:** Think of the particular situations that you have already prayed about. Write those situations below. After writing them, pray over them immediately. Then, before your day ends, pray *again*. Document the times you spend in prayer.

Lord, I come to you concerning

_____
_____
_____
_____
_____
_____
_____
_____
_____
_____
_____
_____

First Prayer - Time: _____ AM/PM

Second Prayer - Time: _____ AM/PM

Third Prayer - Time: _____ AM/PM

# Month 7 | Day 8

**Fast:** No Meat

**Devotion:** Matthew 26:45-46 (ESV) "⁴⁵Then he came to the disciples and said to them, "Sleep and take your rest later on. See, the hour is at hand, and the Son of Man is betrayed into the hands of sinners. ⁴⁶Rise, let us be going; see, my betrayer is at hand.""

---

Martin Cooper said, "Time is precious. Don't throw it away." After Jesus prays the third time, He tells the disciples, "Sleep and take your rest later. The hour is at hand…." Christ knew what was about to occur; therefore, time was precious. Furthermore, in verse 46, Jesus declares, "Rise, let us be going; see, my betrayer is at hand." Jesus did not shy away from what He knew He had to face. These two verses seem to suggest that our Lord was in a hurry to do the will of His Father! After praying three times concerning the same thing and denying His own will, Jesus did not want to waste any more time. He wanted God's will! He accepted God's will.

**Prayer:** Heavenly Father, I thank You for sending Your son Jesus to be the perfect example that I need. I also thank You for every day of my life. Father, I thank You for my challenging days. As I continue to deny my will, help me to accept Your will no matter how hard it may seem. Despite it all, my bad days are much less than my good days. Father, I thank You for the strength to not only accept the challenging days ahead but also to remember that You are with me and will never leave me. In Jesus' name. Amen.

## WEAK BUT WILLING

**Activity:** We all have activities or responsibilities that we look forward to doing or do not look forward to doing. Below, write the things that you look forward to doing as well as the things you do not look forward to doing. As you concentrate on the things you do not look forward to doing but know you need to do, ask God to give you the strength to do them. As you complete those tasks, check them off of your list below.

Things I look forward to doing:

1. _____
2. _____
3. _____
4. _____
5. _____
6. _____

Things I do not look forward to doing, that I know I need to do:

1. _____
2. _____
3. _____
4. _____
5. _____
6. _____

# MONTH 8

## Stay Connected

*The Business of the Mind*

John Chapter 15 and verse 1 states, "I am the true vine, and my father is the vinedresser." It is essential to know that the Word of God speaks of agriculture. For instance, in Isaiah chapter 5 and verse 1, the Bible says, "Let me sing for my beloved my love-song concerning his vineyard." Here, the Prophet Isaiah speaks of Israel as God's vineyard. Therefore, Jesus is the true vine, and God is the vinedresser, the One who cultivates and keeps the vineyard, and we must remain connected. This month, we will spend five days reading the first 17 verses in John chapter 15. As we devote ourselves to this month's devotions, I challenge you to seek God while intentionally allowing Him to be your vinedresser.

# Month 8 | Day 1

**Fast:** No Sweets

**Devotion:** John 15:1-3 (ESV) "¹I am the true vine, and my father is the vinedresser. ²Every branch in me that does not bear fruit he takes away, and every branch that does bear fruit he prunes, that it may bear more fruit. ³Already you are clean because of the word that I have spoken to you."

---

"I am" refers to Christ Jesus. The Bible declares seven (7) "I am" statements concerning Christ. Jesus:

- "I **am** the Bread of Life." John 6:35
- "I **am** the Light of the World." John 8:12
- "I **am** the Door." John 10:9
- "I **am** the Good Shepherd." John 10:11,14
- "I **am** the Resurrection and the Life." John 11:25
- "I **am** the Way and the Truth and the Life." in John 14:6

And lastly, in John 15:1,5, He says, "I **am** the vine."

The scriptures describe the various functions of Jesus, and our connection to Him is necessary. If we disconnect from this vine, the results will be detrimental. One of the most valuable devices for most people is the mobile phone. When the device is connected to its charger, connected to its power source, the mobile phone receives the charge it needs to function and serve its purpose. However, when the phone of your choice is disconnected from the source of power, it may hold a charge for some time; but eventually, the battery will die. The device will not be usable as long as it is dead. It is only beneficial when it is connected to the power source and the battery has had enough time to charge.

Are you connected to the true vine? How often do you disconnect from Him, become drained, and realize a reconnection is needed? Being connected to our Savior is the most important relationship we need.

**Activity:** When our mobile device has been connected to the power source and charged, it can serve its purpose. Below, write the various functions of your mobile device and how you use it throughout the course of your day – after it has been charged due to its connection to the source of power. Then, write how you can impact the Kingdom of God as you stay connected to the true vine.

Benefits of a mobile device after being connected to its source of power:

_____
_____
_____
_____

Benefits of you connecting to the true vine:

_____
_____
_____
_____

**Verse 2 Reflection:**

When I was a child, I was taught Sunday School by a teacher who had a pear tree in her yard. How did I know it was a pear tree? Because I could visibly see the pears hanging from the tree. In verse 2, each branch should bear fruit. Then, each branch should bear more fruit. How fruitful are you? What kind of fruit do you bear?

**Activity:** Follow the directions below.
List the fruit (characteristics of Christ) that you currently bear:
1. _____
2. _____
3. _____

List the fruit (characteristics of Christ) that you do not bear, but need to:
1. _____
2. _____
3. _____

**Prayer:** Lord, I praise You for who You are and for being *the vine*. Because of You and my connection to You, I am alive. Forgive me for the times that I tried to disconnect from You. Because of Your love, You never cut me off, and I thank You for it. In Jesus' name. Amen.

# Month 8 | Day 2

**Fast:** No Sweets

**Devotion:** John 15:4-6 (ESV) "⁴Abide in me, and I in you. As the branch cannot bear fruit by itself, unless it abides in the vine, neither can you, unless you abide in me. ⁵I am the vine; you are the branches. Whoever abides in me and I in him, he it is that bears much fruit, for apart from me you can do nothing. ⁶If anyone does not abide in me, he is thrown away like a branch and withers; and the branches are gathered, thrown into the fire, and burned."

---

Verses 4 and 5 give the results of abiding in Jesus, the true vine. Verse 4 states, "Abide in me and I in you." We will be fruitful when we remain in Christ and He in us. Verse 5 says, "Whoever abides in me and I in him…" Remember, Jesus is the vine, and we bear much fruit in Him. Verse 6 gives the consequences of not abiding in Him:

1. We are thrown away. Once we are disconnected, we are powerless.
2. Like a branch, we wither. Withering happens over some time and is a slow process that takes life.
3. Thrown into the fire and burned. This is equivalent to death. When we disconnect from the vine, we eventually die. Therefore, stay connected to the true vine and LIVE!

**Activity:** Continue to fast from all foods with added sugar, sweets, and junk foods. If the desire for sugar arises, only eat fruit.

## STAY CONNECTED

**Prayer:** Father, I am grateful for Your work in my life through Your Son, Jesus. Without You, I am nothing. Father, as I take my journey through life, I need the power of Your Holy Spirit to aid me in staying connected to You, and I will live for You each day. In Jesus' name. Amen.

# Month 8 | Day 3

**Fast:** No Sweets

**Devotion:** John 15:7-11 (ESV) "⁷If you abide in me, and my words abide in you, ask whatever you wish, and it will be done for you." ⁸By this my Father is glorified, that you bear much fruit and so prove to be my disciples. ⁹As the Father has loved me, so have I loved you. Abide in my love. ¹⁰If you keep my commandments, you will abide in my love, just as I have kept my father's commandments and abide in his love. ¹¹These things I have spoken to you, that my joy may be in you, and that your joy may be full."

The continuation of living in Jesus is necessary! And as you abide in Him and His Words continues to abide in you, you then have the permission to ask whatever you wish (if your requests line up with God's Word), and He will bless you.

**Activity:** As you abide in Jesus, your prayers will be answered. Below make a list of answered prayers. This will serve as a reminder of the importance of staying in Christ.

_____

_____

_____

_____

_____

_____

# Month 8 | Day 4

**Fast:** No Sweets

**Devotion:** John 15:12-15 (ESV) "[12]This is my commandment, that you love one another as I have loved you. [13]Greater love has no one than this that someone lay down his life for his friends. [14]You are my friends if you do what I command you. [15]No longer do I call you servants,[a] for the servant does not know what his master is doing; but I have called you friends, for all that I have heard from my Father I have made known to you."

There are four ideas to take from the above verses:

1. Love one another as Christ loves you.
2. Prefer others above yourself.
3. Your relationship to Christ is based on doing as He says.
4. Our Lord and Savior calls you friend and has shared with you what His Father has shared with Him.

**Prayer:** Lord, I want to thank You for Your commands of love, that You call me friend, and for sharing with me the beautiful things that Your Father has said about me. I am not worthy! Therefore, I honor You, love You, and serve You. I owe You my life. In the name of Jesus, I pray. Amen.

# Month 8 | Day 5

**Fast:** No Sweets

**Devotion:** John 15:16-17 (ESV) "[16]You did not choose Me, but I chose you and appointed you that you should go and bear fruit and that your fruit should abide, so that whatever you ask the Father in my name, he may give it to you. [17]These things I command you so that you will love one another."

---

Many times, our human nature leans toward everything but God. Although you may not have chosen Jesus first, He still chose you. You were selected from the very moment you entered the Earth. Not only did Christ choose you, but He also appointed you to bear fruit. Once you bear fruit, you then earn the blessing to ask for whatever you desire, and it will be given to you.

Obey the command and love one another. Love goes beyond race, social status, culture, backgrounds, neighborhoods, careers, and anything else that is used to separate and divide.

**Activity:** This month was about *Staying Connected*. Below, list consequences of disconnecting from Christ: You may conclude your fast at a designated time today. If you feel led to continue the fast, feel free to do so.

_____

_____

_____

_____

# MONTH 9

# Living It

*The Business of the Mind*

One of the most influential books I have ever read is *Kingdom Man*, written by Dr. Tony Evans. In this writing, Evans teaches his readers the Kingdom Agenda. The Kingdom Agenda is defined as the visible manifestation of the comprehensive rule of God over every area of life. As believers, we should desire not only to please God but to trust Him in each aspect of our being. It is no secret that life can be challenging regarding finances, family, friends, and our faith. However, we must continue to rely on our Heavenly Father for everything we need. The Bible says, "Trust in the Lord with all your heart, and do not lean on your own understanding. In all your ways acknowledge him, and he will make straight your path" (Proverbs 3:5,6 ESV).

This month's devotions will focus on James 5:1-20. The book of James is filled with great wisdom related to living as a Christian. As we continue *Living It* – that is living the life of a Christian – it is important to do three things:

1. Have our priorities in the proper perspective
2. Have patience in trials
3. Continue praying in faith

# Month 9 | Day 1

**Fast:** No Bread

**Devotion:** James 5:1-6 "Come now, you rich, weep and howl for the miseries that are coming upon you. Your riches have rotted, and your garments are moth-eaten. Your gold and silver have corroded, and their corrosion will be evidence against you and will eat your flesh like fire. You have laid up treasure in the last days. Behold, the wages of the laborers who mowed your fields, which you kept back by fraud, are crying out against you, and the cries of the harvesters have reached the ears of the Lord of hosts. You have lived on the earth in luxury and self-indulgence. You have fattened your hearts in a day of slaughter. You have condemned and murdered the righteous person. He does not resist you."

---

**Living It Rich or Living It Right**

It is no secret that finances are an essential part of life, and we need money to live. For most people, becoming rich would be welcomed. However, which is more critical: Living rich or living right? According to scripture, material things will not last. Therefore, our hope should be built on Jesus and pleasing Him. To be clear, it is not a sin to be financially wealthy. Believers go wrong when they prioritize wealth before God. That should never happen. Matthew 6:33 says, "But seek first the kingdom of God and his righteousness, and all these things will be added to you." *These things* refer to the necessities needed for daily life.

Continue to trust God for all your needs. And as you *live it right* by trusting God, working hard, tithing, managing your finances well while also treating others right, you can still gain financial wealth and live a comfortable life. Remember, *living it right* supersedes *living it rich*!

**Activity:** In today's scripture reading, the writer warns the rich.

What does he tell us happens to the riches? _____
_____

What happens to the garments? _____
_____

What happens to the gold and silver? _____
_____

List the things that are most important to you other than financial gain: _____
_____
_____
_____
_____
_____
_____

Be a financial blessing to your local church, family member, friend, or stranger!

**Prayer:** Father, I thank You for everything You have blessed me with. I also honor You with my finances regularly. Lord, as You continue to provide for me and bless me with the desires of my heart, help me to continue to walk in humility, preferring others above myself. I know it is only because of You that I am blessed. Thank You, Lord, for all Your blessings. In Jesus' name. Amen.

# Month 9 | Day 2

**Fast:** No Sweets

**Devotion:** James 5:7-10 "Be patient, therefore, brothers, until the coming of the Lord. See how the farmer waits for the precious fruit of the earth, being patient about it until it receives the early and the late rains. You also be patient. Establish your hearts, for the coming of the Lord is at hand. Do not grumble against one another, brothers, so that you may not be judged; behold, the Judge is standing at the door. As an example of suffering and patience, brothers, take the prophets who spoke in the name of the Lord."

---

**Living It Through the Power of Patience**

At the age of about ten years old, I planted watermelon seeds in the backyard of our family home. Every day I went outside to the spot where the seeds were. I was so excited with anticipation until I expected the watermelon to come up almost immediately. Each day I saw nothing. Due to my immaturity, I had no idea that seeds needed time to grow, and it would not happen in a day or two. How often do we expect an immediate return displaying little to no patience? Throughout life, we must realize that patience is necessary. Romans 12:12 ESV says, "Rejoice in hope, be patient in tribulation, be constant in prayer."

Activity: What are some instances where you have lived the act of exercising patience: _____

_____

# LIVING IT

(cont.) _____

_____
_____
_____
_____
_____
_____
_____
_____

What areas in your life are you currently struggling in the area of having patience: _____

_____
_____
_____
_____
_____
_____
_____
_____

Give the above-written areas to God and allow Him to work them out!

**Prayer:** Father, I thank You for being God. You are God alone. While I exercise patience, I ask that You continue to comfort me and guide me. I thank You for the gift of patience. I will continue to praise Your name while I live! In Jesus' name. Amen.

# Month 9 | Day 3

**Fast:** No Sweets

**Devotion:** James 5:11-12 "Behold, we consider those blessed who remained steadfast. You have heard of the steadfastness of Job, and you have seen the purpose of the Lord, how the Lord is compassionate and merciful. But above all, my brothers, do not swear, either by heaven or by earth or by any other oath, but let your "yes" be yes and your "no" be no, so that you may not fall under condemnation."

## Living It Steadfast

Do you want to be blessed? I am sure your answer is, "YES!" We all desire the blessings of the Lord. Much like earthly fathers wish to bless their children, the Heavenly Father also wants to bless His children. Although we *Live It*, things will be challenging at times, we must first remain steadfast. Biblically, the words *established*, *firm*, and *strengthening* can define steadfast. The Word of God declares in 1 Corinthians 15:58, "Therefore, my beloved brothers, be steadfast, immovable, always abounding in the work of the Lord, knowing that in the Lord your labor is not in vain" (ESV). As we *Live It* through tests, trials, and triumphs, we should remain steadfast as Job did. Secondly, while we *live* steadfastly, we should also use appropriate, positive language. This will ensure that we are consistent in our daily walk with the Lord.

LIVING IT

**Activity:** In what areas are you steadfast (established, firm, strengthened)? _____

_____
_____
_____
_____
_____
_____
_____
_____
_____
_____
_____
_____

Continue to capitalize on these areas and give your areas of weakness to God!

**Prayer:** Lord, I thank You for Your strength. I know You will continue to establish me in every area of my life as I serve You. Thank You, Lord, for the grace and favor to be steadfast and to also speak well of my life! In Jesus' name. Amen.

# Month 9 | Day 4

**Fast:** No Sweets

**Devotion:** James 5:13-15 "Is anyone among you suffering? Let him pray. Is anyone cheerful? Let him sing praise. Is anyone among you sick? Let him call for the elders of the church, and let them pray over him, anointing him with oil in the name of the Lord. And the prayer of faith will save the one who is sick, and the Lord will raise him. And if he has committed sins, he will be forgiven."

**Living It Through the Prayer of Faith**

While Living It, we will experience suffering, cheer (joy), and sickness. However, as you continue to trust God and *Live It* by faith, you will be victorious. Faith is vital to our Christian walk! Hebrews 11:1-3a ESV says, "Now faith is the assurance of things hoped for, the conviction of things not seen. For by it, the people of old received their commendation. By faith, we understand that the word of God created the universe." Faith, as we see it, is a necessity. Partner faith with prayer, and you are destined to experience the joy of the Lord!

**Activity:** This scripture text, James 5:13-15, gives us instructions very plainly in three different areas. Fill in the blanks:

1. Instructions for suffering: Let him _____
2. Instructions for being cheerful: Let him _____
3. Instructions for the sick: Call for the _____ and let them _____ anointing you with oil in the name of the Lord.

4. The Prayer of Faith will

_____

_____

_____

_____

_____

**Prayer:** Lord, I want to thank You for all You have been and done for me. You are my healer, my joy, and my hope! No matter what comes my way, I will put my faith in You as I continue praying to You for all my needs. Lord, I trust You. In Jesus' name. Amen.

# Month 9 | Day 5

**Fast:** No Sweets

**Devotion:** James 5:16-20 "Therefore, confess your sins to one another and pray for one another that you may be healed. The prayer of a righteous person has great power as it is working. Elijah was a man with a nature like ours, and he prayed fervently that it might not rain, and for three years and six months it, did not rain on the earth. Then he prayed again, and the heaven gave rain, and the earth bore its fruit. My brothers, if anyone among you wanders from the truth and someone brings him back, let him know that whoever brings back a sinner from his wandering will save his soul from death and will cover a multitude of sins."

---

This passage of scripture is practical and powerful. There are two practical things that I want to mention: Confession and Praying for one another. Confessing is defined as an acknowledgment of sin to God. The writer in the todays reading also suggests confessing to other people. However, God is, ultimately, our judge. The next practical thing is praying for one another. As a body of believers, connecting in prayer with like-minded believers is essential and strengthening. Prayer not only connects believers, but Prayer also moves God as Elijah did! Never doubt the power of prayer.

**Activity:**

The _____ of a righteous _____ has great _____ as it is working.

## LIVING IT

_____ was a man with a nature like ours, and he _____ _____ that it might not rain, and for _____ _____ and six months it did not _____ on the earth. Then he _____ again, and heaven gave _____, and the earth bore its _____.

My brothers, if anyone among you wanders from the truth and someone brings him back, let him know that whoever brings back a_____ from his wandering will _____ his _____ from _____ and will cover a _____ of _____.

**Prayer:** Father, I thank You for the opportunity of confession, the blessings of the righteous, and healing. Help me always to have a confessing heart that does not judge others. Lord, I am forever grateful for Your forgiveness and love. In Jesus' name. Amen.

# MONTH 10

## Process before Purpose

*The Business of the Mind*

Are you a dreamer? The word *dream* is defined as "a series of thoughts, images, and sensations occurring in a person's mind during sleep." Another definition is "a cherished aspiration, ambition, or ideal." I have had dreams that were noticeably clear and meaningful. There have been other times where my dreams were not so clear or meaningful, however. Dreams can possess a message God wants to relay as a sign or warning. Dreams can also be influenced by Satan, our own emotions, and our personal experiences.

In this month's devotions (Genesis 37, 39, 40 – 50), the Biblical figure, Joseph, has dreams. His dreams were messages providing him a sneak-peak at the plans God had for him. Little did Joseph know; he would live through a painful process that would eventually catapult him to his purpose and promise.

As you engage in this month's devotions, I encourage you to fast during the day and eat only in the evenings, fast from all liquids drinking only water, or stay logged out of your social media accounts. You get to choose one of the three options, if not all three as we read about the process that leads to Joseph's purpose.

# Month 10 | Day 1

**Fast:** You can choose to fast during the day and eat only in the evening, fast from all liquids drinking only water, or take a break and fast from social media.

**Devotion:** Genesis 37:2-4 "²…Joseph, being seventeen years old, was pasturing the flock with his brothers. He was a boy with the sons of Bilhah and Zilpah, his father's wives. And Joseph brought a bad report of them to their father. ³Now Israel loved Joseph more than any other of his sons because he was the son of his old age. And he made him a robe of many colors. ⁴But when his brothers saw that their father loved him more than all his brothers, they hated him and could not speak peacefully to him."

---

Amazingly, Israel fathers Joseph in his old age. Therefore, Joseph is incredibly special to him. Naturally, this favoritism from Israel towards Joseph causes issues amongst Joseph and his brothers. Joseph's siblings despise and hate him. Isn't it funny how one person can love you wholeheartedly, and others hate you vigorously? Joseph experienced extreme love from his earthly father that was very strong, but it also made Joseph a target!

Israel's heavily weighed love for Joseph began a process in the life of Joseph that would affect him for many years. The Process Begins: Joseph is favored by his father.

**Activity:** Why did Israel love Joseph so much? _____

_____

_____

(cont.) _____
_____

How was Joseph shown love by his father? _____
_____
_____
_____

Define Favoritism in your own words: _____
_____
_____
_____

Has anyone shown you favoritism? If so, how? _____
_____
_____
_____

Is favoritism from parents towards a particular child a good thing? Yes [ ] No [ ]

Although challenging, continue to thank God for what He has allowed to happen in your life. And remember, all of us are special to God. Also, if you are a parent, do your best to love each of your children equally without favoritism.

**Prayer:** Heavenly Father, I thank You for my parents. I thank You for choosing them to raise me. Continue to bless my parents. Heavenly Father, help me be the parent You want me to be. Also, Father grant me the strength and wisdom to be the parent my child(ren) need(s). If I am showing favoritism to any of my children, show me. Forgive me. Help me to love my children unconditionally and equally. I cannot do this without You, Father. In Jesus' name. Amen.

## Month 10 | Day 2

**Fast:** You can choose to fast during the day and eat only in the evening, fast from all liquids drinking only water, or take a break and fast from social media.

**Devotion:** Genesis 37:5-9 "Now Joseph had a dream, and when he told it to his brothers, they hated him even more. He said to them, "Hear this dream that I have dreamed: Behold, we were binding sheaves in the field, and behold, my sheaf arose and stood upright. And behold, your sheaves gathered around it and bowed down to my sheaf." His brothers said to him, "Are you indeed to reign over us? Or are you indeed to rule over us?" So, they hated him even more for his dreams and words. Then he dreamed another dream, told it to his brothers, and said, "Behold, I have dreamed another dream. Behold, the sun, the moon, and eleven stars were bowing down to me."

---

**The Process Begins:** Joseph is hated by his brothers… even more. Have you ever said, "I hate eating that" or "I hate drinking that" or "I hate those cars"? Hating a particular food, drink, or automobile is one thing. None of these things are detrimental to life. However, hating an individual is serious. Even more so, hating a sibling is serious. The Bible says Joseph's brothers hated him more and more. Why? Because of the love that is shown to him by their father, Israel, and Joseph's dreams.

Do you have dreams? Dreams that show the favor of God in your life. If so, can you share your dreams with anyone? Can someone share their dreams with you? Are you capable of cheering and supporting others in their dreams? We all should desire to live a better quality of life. We should also want the same for our loved ones.

**Activity:** We are familiar with Joseph and his father, Israel. Can you name Joseph's brothers? Below, fill in the blanks to complete each name. *The answer key is at the end of this chapter.*

S__me__n          _ev__
Ze__ __lun        I__sach__ __
D__n              _a_
As__ __r          N__ph__al__
Re__b__ __        J__ __ ah
B__nj__ am__ __n

**Prayer:** Heavenly Father, I thank You for all that You are to me. I know that You are sovereign and in control of my life, and I desire to honor You. Father, I ask that You bless my family (mother, father, sisters, brothers). Bless them spiritually, naturally, emotionally, and financially. Satan, the Lord, rebukes division and favoritism in my family. I also thank You for the grace to live in love, unity, and peace within my own family. In Jesus' name. Amen.

On the next page, list your family members, and continue praying for everyone you listed.

# THE BUSINESS OF THE MIND

# Month 10 | Day 3

**Fast:** You can choose to fast during the day and eat only in the evening, fast from all liquids drinking only water, or take a break and fast from social media.

**Devotion:** Genesis 37:25-28, 36 "$^{25}$Then they sat down to eat. And looking up, they saw a caravan of Ishmaelites coming from Gilead, with their camels bearing gum, balm, and myrrh, on their way to carry it down to Egypt. $^{26}$Then Judah said to his brothers, "What profit is it if we kill our brother and conceal his blood? $^{27}$Come, let us sell him to the Ishmaelites, and let not our hand be upon him, for he is our brother, our flesh." And his brothers listened to him. $^{28}$Then Midianite traders passed by. And they drew Joseph up and lifted him out of the pit and sold him to the Ishmaelites for twenty shekels of silver. They took Joseph to Egypt. $^{36}$Meanwhile, the Midianites had sold him in Egypt to Potiphar, an officer of Pharaoh, the captain of the guard."

---

**The Process Begins:** Joseph is sold by his brothers

In the year 2004, my wife and I purchased our first home. In 2018, we were blessed to buy our second home. These homes were available to buy because the owners decided to place them on the market. Not only have we purchased homes, but we have also purchased automobiles, clothes, shoes, books, furniture, and many other things. We have played the role of buyer, and in some instances, we have played the role of seller. However, buying and selling material things is different from buying and selling of a person.

Joseph's brothers initially wanted to kill him. Thankfully, one of his brothers, Judah, suggested selling Joseph to the Ishmaelites instead. For Joseph to witness his blood brothers sell him for twenty shekels of silver had to be very disheartening! It was the ultimate betrayal. I have heard it said many times, "It's the people who are close to you that can hurt you!" Joseph's only mistake was telling his family the dreams he had. The favoritism from his father was not his fault. He had nothing to do with his birth order and being born in his dad's old age. Therefore, his brothers getting rid of him was, more than likely, very painful. However, we will discover that this painful process would develop into Joseph's purpose, not only for him but for his family also.

**Activity:** Read Chapter 37 in its entirety. Continue fasting while praying for your family and close friends throughout the day. Yes, pray for those that have *sold you* or have nothing to do with you. Pray for those that have caused your deepest pain.

Was there ever a time when you felt betrayed by loved ones?
Yes [ ] No [ ]

If you answered "Yes," how did that make you feel?
_____
_____
_____
_____
_____

# THE BUSINESS OF THE MIND

How did you grow from the betrayal?

_____

_____

_____

_____

_____

_____

_____

_____

If loved ones have betrayed you, pray for them now. If you cannot pray for them now, make this a goal for the near future.

**Prayer:** Heavenly Father, I come to You at this moment needing Your help and strength. Without You, I am nothing. Father, I thank You for all You are to me and all You provide. Lord, even in the tough times of life's journey, I know You are with me. You will never leave me. Father, I ask You to touch my heart so that I will not be the same as my enemies. I desire to be different from them. Please give me a heart of flesh and not of stone. I give You the glory, honor, and praise. In Jesus' name. Amen.

## Month 10 | Day 4

**Fast:** You can choose to fast during the day and eat only in the evening, fast from all liquids drinking only water, or take a break and fast from social media.

**Devotion:** Genesis 39:2, 39:21, 39:23

²The LORD was with Joseph, and he became a successful man, and he was in the house of his Egyptian master.

²¹ But the LORD was with Joseph and showed him steadfast love and gave him favor in the sight of the keeper of the prison.

²³The keeper of the prison paid no attention to anything that was in Joseph's charge because the LORD was with him. And whatever he did, the LORD made it succeed.

---

**The Process Leads to Promotion**

What a painful experience it must have been for Joseph to witness the betrayal from his flesh and blood brothers! Let us take note of some facts from this historical account:

1. Joseph is only a teenager.
2. His father favors Joseph, and this is no fault of his own.
3. Joseph's brothers hate him.
4. Joseph shares his dreams with his brothers, and they hate him even more.
5. Joseph is sold by his brothers.

Can you imagine being a teenager sold to strangers and not knowing what will happen to you? Joseph's everyday life was snatched from him in a matter of moments. However, the process leads to promotion. Genesis 37 tells how Joseph is punished by his brothers. Genesis 39 allows us to see his promotion despite the harsh treatment.

Are you facing betrayal by people you love? Have you been wronged while doing nothing intentionally to reap the punishment? If so, you are facing the same dilemma as Joseph. Nevertheless, hang in there! Stay positive. Stay humble. God will work it out!

Below are a few verses that stand out. If we are not careful, negativity will be the only part of Joseph's life that we will pay attention to. While these misfortunes are essential to note and remember, they are not the end of Joseph's life because the Lord was with Joseph.

Three important things happen to Joseph in this story. First, Joseph is promoted to the overseer of Potiphar's house and in charge of all he has. Secondly, Joseph is falsely accused of seducing his master's wife. Lastly, because of the accusation, which is entirely not true, Joseph is thrown into prison. Joseph goes from low to high and back to low again. Nonetheless, while in prison, the Lord was with Joseph. Remember, even in your darkest moments; the Lord is with you! Throughout life's journey, we will face challenges, but Hebrews 13:5b (ESV) says, "...I will never leave you nor forsake you." Also, Hebrews 13:6 (ESV) declares, "So we can confidently say, the Lord is my helper; I will not fear; what can man do to me?" Whatever you are facing at this very hour, keep in mind, the Lord is with you through it all!

THE BUSINESS OF THE MIND

**Activity:** Read Chapter 39 in its entirety. This will give you the complete picture of the happenings in Joseph's life in this reading.

In the spaces provided below, write the personal circumstances you have faced in the first column. In the second column, document how the Lord proved He was with you.

| My Circumstance | How the Lord proved He was with me |
|---|---|
|  |  |
|  |  |
|  |  |
|  |  |
|  |  |
|  |  |
|  |  |
|  |  |

# Month 10 | Day 5

**Fast:** You can choose to fast during the day and eat only in the evening, fast from all liquids drinking only water, or take a break and fast from social media.

**Devotion:** Genesis 40:5-8 [5]And one night they both dreamed—the cupbearer and the baker of the king of Egypt, who were confined in prison—each his dream, and each dream with its interpretation. [6]When Joseph came to them in the morning, he saw that they were troubled. [7]So, he asked Pharaoh's officers who were with him in custody in his master's house, ``Why are your faces downcast today?'' [8]They said to him, ``We have had dreams, and there is no one to interpret them.'' And Joseph said to them, "Do not interpretations belong to God? Please tell them to me."

---

**Joseph Serves While in Prison**

The year was 2016. I was employed by a good company with great pay and benefits. I had a company truck, gas card, and mobile phone. This company also provided the expensive steel-toe boots that were required. Those benefits, although significant, did not stop me from absolutely hating the daily operations that my job as a technician required. I hated going to work! The weather conditions were important to me because this was outdoor plant work. It was not a *9 to 5* office job. The average hours worked could range from 45-70 hours per week. However, supporting my family was my motivation. Therefore, I did what I had to do. On one day, the weather was not favorable. It was freezing cold, and it rained all day long. As I walked through the building gathering materials to put in my work truck, the manager (who was the supervisor to my direct supervisor) said to me, "How is the weather out there today?" I, in turn, replied, "It's freezing and rainy today!" The manager then responded to me, "Oh really? I thought it was 72 degrees and sunny!" Not knowing what he meant (I had not been employed but a few weeks), I disagreed with him immediately! The manager looked at me while laughing and said, "In this business, it is always 72 degrees and sunny no matter what the weather is!" I understood then that work needed to be completed no matter the weather conditions. I had to fix my mind to believe it was 72 degrees and sunny. It was all about having a good attitude and serving its customers no matter what!

In this chapter, Joseph is in prison. He is approached by two individuals who need their dream interpreted. I love what Joseph says to them. In Genesis chapter 40 and verse 8, he says, "Do not interpretations belong to God? Please tell them to me." Joseph had previously shared his dreams with his brothers and father, so he was accustomed to dreams. Joseph also trusted that God would give him the interpretation of the cupbearer and baker's dreams. The two men share their dreams with Joseph, and he interprets them. This is significant because before Joseph was put in prison, he served and used his gift to oversee his master's home and property. He could have had sex with his master's wife, but he refused. Joseph displayed a solid work ethic as well as integrity before prison. After being placed in jail, he continued to be a blessing to others. As the manager of the previous company that I worked for, Joseph had a *72 degrees and sunny attitude.*

He could have chosen not to assist the cupbearer and baker with the interpretation of the dreams. He could have been antisocial towards them due to his struggle. He was in prison and had not done anything wrong. Nonetheless, Joseph allowed God to use him to help others despite his suffering.

I encourage you to keep that *72 degrees and sunny attitude*. Joseph did it while in prison. Indeed, God will give us the grace to do it while in our home, job, community, and church.

**Activity:** The next devotional will cover Genesis 50. You can move along to this devotional tomorrow, but I encourage you to take the next few days to read Genesis chapters 41-49.

| Genesis 41 | Genesis 42 | Genesis 43 |
| Genesis 44 | Genesis 45 | Genesis 46 |
| Genesis 47 | Genesis 48 | Genesis 49 |

# Month 10 | Day 6

**Fast:** You can choose to fast during the day and eat only in the evening, fast from all liquids drinking only water, or take a break and fast from social media.

**Devotion:** Genesis 50: 15-21 "[15]When Joseph's brothers saw that their father was dead, they said, "It may be that Joseph will hate us and pay us back for all the evil that we did to him." [16]So, they sent a message to Joseph, saying, "Your father gave this command before he died: [17]"Say to Joseph, "Please forgive the transgression of your brothers and their sin, because they did evil to you."" And now, please forgive the transgression of the servants of the God your father." Joseph wept when they spoke to him. [18]His brothers also came and fell before him and said, "Behold, we are your servants."

[19]But Joseph said to them, "Do not fear, for am I in the place of God? [20]As for you, you meant evil against me, but God meant it for good, to bring it about that many people should be kept alive, as they are today. [21]So do not fear; I will provide for you and your little ones." Thus, he comforted them and spoke kindly to them."

---

## The Process Leads to Joseph's Purpose

There is no doubt Joseph's life had a great purpose. However, before he could achieve his goal, he encountered several processes. Let us look at this again.

- Joseph is favored by his father.
- Joseph is hated by his brothers.
- Joseph is hated even more by his brothers.

- Joseph is sold.
- Joseph is sold again.
- Joseph is made overseer of Potiphar's house.
- Potiphar's wife falsely accuses Joseph.
- Joseph is imprisoned because of the false accusation.
- Joseph then interprets the dreams of the cupbearer and baker.
- Joseph helps the cupbearer and baker, but once freed from prison, the cupbearer does not return the favor. Joseph remains in jail.
- Joseph interprets Pharaoh's dreams and is promoted to power over Pharaoh's house and people.
- Joseph uses his rise in power to help his family.

The brothers of Joseph initially plot to kill him, but they decide to sell him instead. Joseph is sold more than once. After Potiphar purchases him, Joseph is made overseer of his house. He is not treated fairly and is put in jail. However, Joseph is wise and favored by God. God will use his life to bless his family. Joseph was a man of authority and power. Once he recognized his brothers, he could have used his position of power to abuse and seek revenge upon his brothers, but he did not. What a fantastic display of forgiveness, humility, and strength! As believers in Christ, we should desire to be the opposite of our enemies.

The scripture text at the end of this paragraph shows Joseph's dreams in action. Not only did Joseph rise to power, but his brothers also bowed to him and declared that they would now serve him. Joseph said one of the most powerful statements I have ever heard: "As for you, you meant evil against me, but God meant it for good..." (Genesis 50:20, ESV).

**Activity:** Read Genesis 50 in its entirety.

Whether you are a mother, father, supervisor, teacher, or director, you are a person of influence and power. Write below how you can positively use your ability to serve others even after being wronged.

I can use my authority and influence to help others by:

_____
_____
_____
_____
_____
_____
_____
_____
_____
_____
_____
_____
_____
_____
_____
_____
_____
_____

# Month 10 | Day 7

**Fast:** You can choose to fast during the day and eat only in the evening, fast from all liquids drinking only water, or take a break and fast from social media.

**Devotion:** Genesis 37, 39-50

---

**Devotional Reflections**

Now that you have read the entire story of Joseph (chapters 37, 39-50), write your thoughts on what Joseph's life experiences mean to you and how you have been impacted.

_____
_____
_____
_____
_____
_____
_____
_____
_____
_____
_____
_____
_____
_____
_____
_____

## PROCESS BEFORE PURPOSE

# THE BUSINESS OF THE MIND

*Day 2, Chapter 37 Answer key: Joseph's brothers:*
**Simeon, Levi, Zebulun, Issachar, Dan, Gad, Asher, Naphtali, Reuben, Judah, and Benjamin.**

# MONTH 11

## Seasons and Assignments

*The Business of the Mind*

There are four seasons: Winter, Spring, Summer, and Fall. My personal favorite is Fall because the temperature is exactly right for me, there are a lot of sunny days, and, of course, football season begins! Each year the seasons change every three months. Regardless of your age, you have witnessed the seasons change year after year. The cycle of nature's changing seasons is anticipated. We expect seasons and can often predict how the temperatures will rise and drop according to our geographical location.

Is there anything in your life that is always predictable? As young children and teenagers, we attended school each August through May. We also enjoyed the summer break; for some came the college years of meeting new people, taking new courses, and attending various functions. Finally, we land the job of our choice, waking up simultaneously and going through the same routine. Our lives can be very monotonous as we do the same things day after day. Careers, relationships, and seasons change every so often. They change repeatedly. Even though seasons and other things change, it is ironic how the same changes occur frequently.

## SEASONS AND ASSIGNMENTS

This month's devotions will come from Ecclesiastes 3:1-8 ESV with verse one saying, "For everything, there is a season and a time for every matter under heaven." This scripture lets us know that seasons change even though life changes are repetitive. As you fast this month from sweets and liquids, drinking only water, be sure to pray throughout each day.

# Month 11 | Day 1

**Fast:** No sweets; water as only beverage

**Devotion:** Ecclesiastes 3:2, "A time to be born, and a time to die; a time to plant, and a time to pluck up what is planted."

**Birth, Death, Plant and Pluck Up**

*Birth* is defined as the emergence of a new individual from the body of its parent. Birth can also mean to give rise to; to originate (Merriam-Webster Dictionary). Therefore, we can birth a variety of things. *Death* is defined as the end of life when someone or something dies; the permanent end of something not alive: the ruin or destruction of something (Merriam-Webster Dictionary). Death not only applies to people. As the definition shows, it also applies to things. To *Plant* means to put (a seed, flower, or plant) in the ground to grow, establish, and institute (Merriam-Webster Dictionary). *Pluck* is to move, remove, or separate forcibly or abruptly (Merriam-Webster Dictionary).

**Activity:** Using the example below, complete the chart on the next page, filling in things you have birthed, things that have experienced death, things you have planted and plucked up in your personal life. Examples have been provided.

| Birth | Death | Plant | Pluck |
|---|---|---|---|
| A non-profit organization | An unhealthy relationship | A Church | An unwanted job |

## SEASONS AND ASSIGNMENTS

| Birth | Death | Plant | Pluck |
|---|---|---|---|
|  |  |  |  |
|  |  |  |  |
|  |  |  |  |
|  |  |  |  |
|  |  |  |  |
|  |  |  |  |
|  |  |  |  |
|  |  |  |  |
|  |  |  |  |
|  |  |  |  |

# Month 11 | Day 2

**Fast:** No sweets; water as only beverage

**Devotion:** Ecclesiastes 3:3, "A time to kill, and a time to heal; a time to break down, and a time to build up."

**Kill, Heal, Build and Break**

*Kill* means to put an end to (Merriam-Webster Dictionary). *Heal* is to make free from injury or disease; to make sound or whole; to make healthy again; to restore to health (Merriam-Webster Dictionary). *Break Down* is defined as failure to progress or have an effect.

To *Build Up* is to promote health, strength, esteem, or reputation.

**Activity:** Below and on the next page, write an example for each column that you need to kill, heal, break down or build up.

| Kill | Heal | Break Down | Build Up |
|---|---|---|---|
| Racial Prejudice | A Broken Heart | Pride | Your Self-Worth |
| | | | |
| | | | |

## SEASONS AND ASSIGNMENTS

| Kill | Heal | Break Down | Build Up |
|------|------|------------|----------|
|      |      |            |          |
|      |      |            |          |
|      |      |            |          |
|      |      |            |          |
|      |      |            |          |
|      |      |            |          |
|      |      |            |          |
|      |      |            |          |
|      |      |            |          |

# Month 11 | Day 3

**Fast:** No sweets; water as only beverage

**Devotion:** Ecclesiastes 3:4 "A time to weep, and a time to laugh; a time to mourn, and a time to dance."

**Weeping, Laughing, Mourning, and Dancing**

Do you remember a time when you experienced weeping, laughing, mourning, and/or dancing as various seasons of your life? Document your experiences.

**Weeping**

_____
_____
_____
_____
_____
_____

**Laughing**

_____
_____
_____
_____
_____
_____

## Mourning



## Dancing

# Month 11 | Day 4

**Fast:** No sweets; water as only beverage

**Devotion:** Ecclesiastes 3:5 "A time to cast away stones, and a time to gather stones together; a time to embrace, and a time to refrain from embracing."

---

**Casting Away:** Document a time you have had to cast away things:

_____
_____
_____
_____
_____


**Gathering:** Write below your personal experiences of gathering things:

_____
_____
_____
_____
_____


**Embracing:** What or who do you embrace?

_____
_____
_____
_____

**Releasing:** Document below people, places, or things you refrain from embracing.

_____

_____

_____

_____

_____

# Month 11 | Day 5

**Fast:** No sweets; water as only beverage

**Devotion:** Ecclesiastes 3:6 "A time to seek, and a time to lose; a time to keep, and a time to cast away."

---

The *Vine's Complete Expository Dictionary of Old and New Testament Words* provides the Biblical definition for each of the following words:

- **Seek** means to find.
- **Lose** is defined as cause to perish; destroy; kill.
- **Keep** means to watch, guard. (Example: "To watch one's mouth." Proverbs 13:3; the tongue, Psalms 34;13).
- **Cast Away** is to throw; to fling.

Our lives consist of natural and spiritual things. On the next page, write one natural and one spiritual thing for each category. For instance: *Seek – Naturally, I seek a better career. Spiritually, I seek ways to please God.*

## Seek

Naturally:

_____

_____

_____

Spiritually:

_____

_____

_____

## Lose

Naturally:

_____

_____

_____

Spiritually:

_____

_____

_____

## Keep

Naturally:

___

___

___


Spiritually:

___

___

___


## Cast Away

Naturally:

___

___

___


Spiritually:

___

___

___

# Month 11 | Day 6

**Fast:** No sweets; water as only beverage

**Devotion:** Ecclesiastes 3:7 "A time to tear, and a time to sew; a time to keep silent, and a time to speak."

---

The *Vine's Complete Expository Dictionary of Old and New Testament* Words provides the Biblical definition of the following words:

- A **tear** is defined as tear; rend; rending garment in grief.
- **Sew** is to sew together, stitch.
- **Keep Silent** means to be silent, inactive, still.
- **Speak** is to talk.

**Activity:** On the next pages, write an example in each column for the season you have experienced a time to keep silent and a season to speak.

## SEASONS AND ASSIGNMENTS

| Keep Silent | Speak |
|---|---|
|  |  |
|  |  |
|  |  |
|  |  |
|  |  |
|  |  |

| Keep Silent | Speak |
| --- | --- |
|  |  |
|  |  |
|  |  |
|  |  |

**Prayer:** Lord, I want to thank You for everything that has taken place in my life. Although every season has not been easy, You have guided me through them all. Father, I need wisdom on when to keep silent and when to speak. Please help me refrain from idle talk and saying things I should not say. Also, Father, help me speak when I know I need to. These things I ask in Your son Jesus' name. Amen.

# Month 11 | Day 7

**Fast:** No sweets; water as only beverage

**Devotion:** Ecclesiastes 3:8 "A time to love, and a time to hate; a time for war, and a time for peace."

---

The definitions below are from *Vine's Complete Expository Dictionary of Old and New Testament Words.*

| Love | Affection both pure & impure, divine & human |
|------|----------------------------------------------|
| Hate | Scorn; Decrease in status |
| War | Battle; Fighting |
| Peace | Completeness, Soundness, Welfare |

*(Whitaker, R., Brown, F., Driver, S. R. (Samuel R., & Briggs, C. A. (Charles A. (1906). The Abridged Brown-Driver-Briggs Hebrew-English Lexicon of the Old Testament: from A Hebrew and English Lexicon of the Old Testament by Francis Brown, S.R. Driver, and Charles Briggs, based on the lexicon of Wilhelm Gesenius. Boston; New York: Houghton, Mifflin, and Company).

**Activity:** Document what/who you love and why; what/who you hate and why. Also, write reasons you believe in war and note the importance of peace.

### Love

Who/What?

_____

_____

_____

_____

_____

Why?

_____

_____

_____

_____

## Hate

Who/What?

_____

_____

_____

_____

Why?

_____

_____

_____

_____

Reasons I believe in War:

_____

_____

_____

The importance of Peace:

_____
_____
_____
_____
_____
_____
_____
_____

**Prayer:** Heavenly Father, I thank You for everything You are for me. In every season and assignment in my life, You are worthy of honor and praise, whether good or bad. I will continue to bless Your name at all times. Father, I love You. In Jesus' name. Amen.

# MONTH 12

## Predestined

*The Business of the Mind*

One of the greatest blessings I have encountered is being a father! In the year 2001, my wife gave birth to our oldest son. Then in 2004, she birthed our second and youngest son. The baby *came to life* during the first pregnancy around 11 pm each night as he would begin kicking and rolling around in the womb. During an ultrasound, we watched as he turned flips! Also, during the second pregnancy, this child hardly moved at all. He would kick, now and then, but the movement was nothing compared to the first baby. Even though these unborn boys were in their mother's womb, we learned their tendencies and times of activity. Although we had not met them face-to-face, we felt we already knew them.

Jeremiah 1:5 ESV says, "Before I formed you in the womb I knew you, and before you were born, I consecrated you; I appointed you a prophet to the nations." Before your mother and father conceived you, God already knew your gender, how you would look, your weight, your length, and your blood type! He knew everything about you! He knew all of us before we knew ourselves. What an amazing God! He also knew the calling you would have on your life. The truth is, He is the One who not only made you but called you to your specific ministry. Your Heavenly Father gifted you naturally and spiritually.

## Month 12 | Day 1

**Fast:** No sweets; water as only beverage

**Devotion:** Jeremiah 1:5a "Before I formed you in the womb, I knew you...."

---

**I Knew You**

A new analysis from the March of Dimes says women are now pregnant for 39 weeks and not 40. God is so powerful that He does not need 39 or 40 weeks to know the baby in the womb. The truth of the matter is that He knew you before you were formed. The reason He knew you before you were formed is that He is the one who formed you. No one knows you better than your creator! The word *form* is a technical potter's word, and it is often used in connection with the potter at work. The Biblical meaning of the word *form(ed)* is a general term of craftsmanship or handiwork (Vine's Complete Expository Dictionary Page 86). This is the same as the initial thought or idea that comes to your mind concerning anything you do. It is in the mind first; then it comes into being. You were in the mind of God being thought about, cared for, and loved on before you were in your mother's womb. What an impressive display of love.

**Activity:** God knew you before He formed you in the womb. How well do you know yourself? Knowing yourself is particularly important. On the next page, write what you know about yourself.

# PREDESTINED

| Positive Things I Know About Myself | Not-so Positive Things I Know About Myself |
|---|---|
| | |

Continue developing the positive things about yourself and ask God to help you with the not-so positive stuff.

**Prayer:** Father, I thank You for forming me; You knew me and knew everything about me. I am Yours. Lord, help me with areas in my life that are not pleasing to You. I desire to please You. In Jesus' name. Amen.

# Month 12 | Day 2

**Fast:** No sweets; water as only beverage

**Devotion:** Jeremiah 1:5b "...and before you were born, I consecrated you."

---

## I Consecrated You

Biblically the word consecrate means to anoint or to ordain. For example, after showing faithfulness in ministry for several years, I was blessed or ordained as an Elder. Then, I was consecrated or ordained as a Pastor. Although men led my consecration, God was solely responsible for calling me. My Heavenly Father knew what I would be. My responsibility was to accept the call He placed upon my life. This verse tells us that God consecrated Jeremiah before he was ever born, and God was indeed serious about Jeremiah's call. You, too, have been called and blessed by God! Your specific calling may be different from Jeremiah's call; however, God knows you! He knows your strengths, weaknesses, gifts, talents, calling, and areas in which you will thrive. It is important to remember that God consecrated Jeremiah, and Jehovah did not need anyone else's approval or opinion. The same works for you! Remember, God is sovereign and all-powerful. It has often been said that God has the "final say." Well, here, God has the "first say."

**Activity:** Read the scriptures on the next page and reflect on them throughout the day.

## PREDESTINED

### Matthew 22:14

For many are called, but few are chosen.

### Romans 8:28-30 ESV

And we know that for those who love God all things work together for good, for those who are called according to his purpose. For those he foreknew, he also predestined to be conformed to the image of his Son so that he might be the firstborn among many brothers. And those whom he predestined he also called, and those whom he called he also justified, and those whom he justified he also glorified.

### Philippians 1:6 ESV

And I am sure of this, that he who began a good work in you will bring it to completion at the day of Jesus Christ.

### 1 Timothy 1:12 ESV

I thank him who has given me strength, Christ Jesus our Lord, because he judged me faithful, appointing me to his service.

### 2 Timothy 1:9 ESV

Who saved us and called us to a holy calling, not because of our works but because of his purpose and grace, which he gave us in Christ Jesus before the ages began.

### 1 Peter 2:9 ESV

But you are a chosen race, a royal priesthood, a holy nation, a people for his possession, that you may proclaim the excellencies of him who called you out of darkness into his marvelous light.

# Month 12 | Day 3

**Fast:** No sweets; water as only beverage

**Devotion:** Jeremiah 1:5c says, "I appointed you a prophet to the nations."

---

## I Appointed You

The basic meaning of *appoint* is to "visit". Another meaning is to "establish or set in authority" (Bible Dictionaries - Baker's Evangelical Dictionary of Biblical Theology). God knew, consecrated, and appointed Jeremiah. This vessel would be appointed *or set in authority* to prophesy and declare what the Lord had spoken to the nations. He would not need the permission or validation of men to walk in his God-given appointment. Often people desire the approval of men more than being established by God. However, the call on Jeremiah's life, and your life, is far mightier than the fanfare of man. And your appointment by God will speak for itself. When your Creator, God, made you, He knew exactly what He was doing. Despite your flaws, failures, habits, and hang-ups, God can still appoint you. He wants to establish you. Remember, He knew you before you were born. Therefore, He knows everything about you. The best part and the worst part of you.

## Activity:

In what area(s) has God appointed, or given you authority?

_____

_____

## PREDESTINED

(cont.) _____
_____
_____
_____

Are you operating in your appointment? Yes _____ No_____

If not, why?
_____
_____
_____
_____
_____
_____
_____

As you finish this month's devotion, read Jeremiah chapter one in its entirety throughout the remainder of the month.

**Prayer:** Father, I give thanks to You for knowing me, consecrating me, and appointing me. Please forgive me for neglecting what I know You have called me to do. I need Your strength to carry me through and Your wisdom to learn how to use my appointment for Your glory. Through Christ, I know I can do all things. In Jesus' name. Amen.

References not noted in the text:

Harris, W. H., III, Ritzema, E., Brannan, R., Mangum, D., Dunham, J., Reimer, J. A., & Wierenga, M. (Eds.). (2012). *The Lexham English Bible* (Ga 5:22–23). Bellingham, WA: Lexham Press. [Month 2 Day 9]

Coleman, Robert (1993). *The Master Plan of Evangelism*. Spire (Revell, a division of Baker Publishing Group).

Evans, Tony (2012). *Kingdom Man*. Tyndale House Publishers. Carol Stream. Illinois

Lynn, Shereen (2011). *The Shepherd's Oil – Equip Her* (equipherlife.com) June 23, 2011

Ellis, Nicky (2020). *The Shepherd's Oil. Why Do Shepherds Put Oil On Sheep?* — Farm & Animals (farmandanimals.com)

Sharpe, Reginald (2015). HOH Macon Pastor Reginald Sharpe Jr. "*Table Talk*"
https://www.youtube.com/watch?v=oibo1UXDBEg

www.ingramcontent.com/pod-product-compliance
Lightning Source LLC
Chambersburg PA
CBHW072157200426
43209CB00079B/1975/J